THIS GREEN EARTH

A Celebration of Nature Poetry

With best wishes from

Ken and Barbara

August 98 :

~THIS GREEN EARTH

A CELEBRATION
of
NATURE POETRY

Edited by
WILLIAM SCAMMELL

Ellenbank
Press

Published by Ellenbank Press
The Lathes
Selby Terrace
Maryport
Cumbria CA15 6LX

First published 1992

Designed by Mary Blood

Typeset in 11/12 Garamond by Ace Filmsetting Ltd, Frome
Printed and bound in Great Britain by Biddles Ltd,
Guildford and King's Lynn

British Library Cataloguing in Publication Data

A catalogue record for this book is available
from the British Library

ISBN 1 873551 04 5

CONTENTS

FISH, FLESH OR FOWL

GREEN THOUGHTS

LOVE IN A LANDSCAPE

ELEMENTS AND SEASONS

FLOWERS, PLANTS AND TREES

INTRODUCTION

On 1 November 1800 Coleridge wrote excitedly to his friend and patron Josiah Wedgwood about the wonderful views from his new house in Keswick:

> The room in which I write commands six distinct landscapes – the two lakes, the vale, the river, and mountains and mists, and clouds, and sunshine make endless combinations, as if heaven and earth were forever talking to each other . . .

That phrase about 'heaven and earth . . . talking to each other' is a useful working description of nature poetry itself, which seeks to mirror the natural world and explore our place within it.

Coleridge's response echoes Shakespeare's comment that 'The poet's eye . . ./Doth glance from heaven to earth, from earth to heaven' (*A Midsummer Night's Dream*, V, i), and enlarges on William Cowper's famous pronouncement in *The Task*: 'God made the country, and man made the town'. It follows from Cowper's remark that in exploring the country the Romantics were also exploring the nature of God, immanent in every rock and tree and blade of grass – 'soul of all my moral being', as Wordsworth put it in 'Tintern Abbey'.

The English love affair with nature goes back a long way, taking different forms at different periods, and reaching its height in the Romantic revolution of 1770–1820. Earlier poets, such as Dr Johnson in his novel *Rasselas*, had argued that the writer's job was to explore the generic rather than to 'number the streaks of the tulip'. Later ones have been apt to argue that our view of nature is as much a cultural construct as it is an account of what is really 'out there'. In his poem 'Mountains', W. H. Auden tries out (and later dismisses) this sceptical and analytical approach to nature: 'Am I/To see in the Lake District, then,/Another bourgeois invention like the piano?'

The modern consensus was perhaps best expressed by Ted Hughes, writing in the *New Statesman* of 2 October 1964:

> The laws of the Creation are the only literally rational things, and we don't yet know what they are. The nearest we can come to rational thinking is to stand respectfully, hat in hand, before this Creation, exceedingly alert for a new word . . .

Nature poetry, explicitly or implicitly, also provides a critique of social and civilised man. We go to, or live in, the countryside not only to escape the pressures of town and workplace but to discover or rediscover what has been lost or buried or falsified by theory and 'progress'. As Tom Paulin says in his book of essays *Minotaur*:

> The nature poet reports back to society from the wild. He does not address us as citizens or preach the civic virtues, nor does he express opinions about public events or political issues. Celebrating a time before history, he is the rhapsodist of the wet and the wilderness, the feral and untamed . . . [He] returns us to the *dei inferii*, to the gods of the underworld and the life of the tribe . . . Yet nature poetry is always a form of disguised social comment. It may face the campfire and the darkness of the cave, but its back is to the daylight . . .

There are some qualifications needed here – I don't think the nature poet is quite so apolitical as Paulin suggests – but the general burden of his argument is surely correct.

In many ways, perhaps in most, our delighted and awestruck responses to nature are identical to those of our ancestors. For all that we sometimes feel bewildered or marginalised by the discoveries of modern science, it is precisely nature which restores to us the innocence we thought irrecoverable. 'There lives the dearest freshness deep down things' says Hopkins. Wordsworth's 'thoughts . . . too deep for tears' are provoked by 'the meanest flower that blows'. Eliot's waste land is redeemed by water, flowers, birds and something of that same 'wise passiveness' advocated by Wordsworth in the Lucy poems, 'The Leech Gatherer' and 'The Prelude'.

'Nature' and its adjective 'natural' are complex words, taking up many columns in the *Oxford English Dictionary* and whole libraries of specialised knowledge. For the earliest men and women, and perhaps for some remote tribes still today, nature was not so much an environment (a word that didn't get itself invented until the nineteenth century, and grew tall with the advent of Darwinism) as the ground of being. Consequently ideas of appreciating, loving, conserving or exploiting it hardly arose. It was simply there, omnipresent and all-powerful, to be propitiated, thanked, obeyed, and co-operated with. 'The force that through the green fuse drives the flower', in Dylan Thomas's famous phrase, was no more detachable from existence than birth or death, and certainly not an object of study.

The decline of religious belief, the rise of science and technology, the growth of the leisure industry, the attempt to quantify and 'manage' everything under the sun, have all played a significant part in the way we look at nature, which now acts also as adventure playground and elixir of mental health, bestowing its healing powers on the battered modern psyche. There are dangers and sentimentalities in this commodification of nature no less than in the exploitation of earth's resources by greedy governments and multinationals. And yet nature remains 'what it always was' (as Eliot said in 'The Dry Salvages'); an index of sanity whose laws are 'the only literally rational things'; endlessly pleasurable, yet 'of ample power to chasten and subdue' (in Wordsworth's 'Tintern Abbey').

Indeed Wordsworth goes on to describe it, in a striking phrase in his great autobiographical poem 'The Prelude', as a scene or drama of 'visionary dreariness' (see page 107). The second term in this searching paradox can easily get obscured in the picture-postcard view of nature peddled by the tourist and heritage industries. Yet Wordsworth's honesty about nature goes hand in hand with his honesty about human nature and its tendency to harden into the orthodoxies of materialism and conventional religion. 'Great God! I'd rather be a pagan . . .' than forever 'getting and spending, lay[ing] waste our powers' (see p. 102), powers we share with the universe at large.

When Hamlet prays this 'too, too solid flesh' to 'melt, thaw, and resolve itself into a dew' he instinctively reaches for 'natural' images, echoing Marvell's equally famous annihilation of the self to a 'green thought in a green shade'. In all these usages nature is not simply to be applied as a balm but entered into, undergone, as corrective for an ego spun out of control.

Language itself tells us a lot about nature and our relationship to it;

also about our attempts to comprehend and write about it.

Consider the process by which a piece of ground becomes a 'territory', a 'county', a 'park'; terrain becomes a 'landscape'; landscape becomes a 'prospect' or 'view'; wilderness is cultivated and tamed for use as garden or farm or nature reserve . . . and you have an analogy for taming the babble of speech into the civil uses of literature. (Indeed the Greeks explicitly compared the 'turn' from one line of verse to the next with the ploughman's turn at the end of the furrow.)

Just as nature-lovers strive to preserve all that is wild and natural, so poets try to put back the primal energies of speech and song and dance into their rhythms and diction. There is a continuous battle or dialectic going on in both spheres between inner and outer, barbarity and civilisation, pagan wildness and preachy ritual, brain and tongue, formality and informality, psychic use and mercantile use, pristine rock and the intensive labour of culture. Poets pack all these complex interactions into the pulses of their verse, and nature poetry can thus be seen as a reflection of the way we are implicated in nature, and of how nature speaks in us.

If nature began as the ground of being, as I suggested earlier, it went on to become a psychic battleground for the Greeks and Romans, an allegory of divine love for early Christians, a heroic backdrop for Renaissance man, a moralised landscape for the Augustans, an electric thrill of revolution and rebirth for the Romantics, a sonorous hymn for the Victorians, and a problematical inheritance for ourselves, who have Faustian powers of technology at our disposal and minds nourished on a never-to-be-forgotten view of the earth floating in space.

In this anthology I have tried to represent some of the best British nature poets from Chaucer to the present, juxtaposing different ages and sensibilities in order to bring out continuities and contrasts. There is humorous, satirical, exasperated poetry as well as the more serious and solemn variety, joyous lyric verse and fabulous topography.

The various categories under which I have gathered the poems are working suggestions rather than watertight compartments.

15

Poems aim at wholeness, not the convenience of the anthologist, and some of them would have been at home in any one of several sections. The proportion of modern and contemporary poems, originally quite high, has had to be tempered by the constraints of a limited budget.

The book begins with poems about specific places, moving around the British Isles from south to north. Next comes a celebration of those 'brilliant creatures' we share the planet with – birds, animals, insects and fish. 'Green Thoughts' brings together a number of classic meditations on nature, mortality and the significance we read into the cycle of growth and decay. 'Love in a Landscape' shows love and some related emotions at work in their natural habitat, where inner and outer weather conditions seem almost indistinguishable one from another. This leads on to 'Elements and Seasons', and finally to 'Flowers, Plants and Trees'.

I have provided short introductions to each of these sections, suggesting ways in which the poems relate to matters of perennial interest. Since words are made out of our own breath, and rhythm arrives with the earliest heartbeat, they speak to us more intimately and more pleasurably than any other form of knowledge. All we have to do is listen.

William Scammell
Aspatria, 1992

LIST OF ILLUSTRATIONS

Acknowledgements

The editor and publishers wish to thank Bloodaxe Books for permission to reprint 'Why Write of the Sun' from *Zoom!* by Simon Armitage (1989); Carcanet Press for 'Driving West' and 'After Death' by Patricia Beer from *Collected Poems* (1988), 'New Year's Day at Lepe' from *A View From the Source* by Jeremy Hooker, and 'By Ferry to the Island' by Iain Crichton Smith from *Selected Poems* (1985); Faber and Faber Ltd for 'The Letter' and 'Roman Wall Blues' by W. H. Auden from *The English Auden* edited by Edward Mendelson, 'Pike' from *Lupercal*, 'The Thought-Fox' from *The Hawk in the Rain*, 'Thistles' and 'Wodwo' from *Wodwo*, all by Ted Hughes, 'Days' from *The Whitsun Weddings* by Philip Larkin, 'Dandelions' from *Collected Poems* by Louis MacNeice, 'The One Desire' from *Selected Poems 1968–1983* by Paul Muldoon, and 'Wuthering Heights' by Sylvia Plath from *Sylvia Plath: Collected Poems* edited by Ted Hughes; Faber and Faber Ltd and Irvine Hunt for 'From a Boat at Coniston' by Norman Nicholson from *Selected Poems 1940–1982*; Martin, Brian & O'Keeffe Ltd for extracts from 'On a Raised Beach' by Hugh MacDiarmid; Sheil Land Associates Ltd for 'Owl', copyright © George Macbeth, 1963, from *The Broken Places* by George Macbeth (Scorpion Press); the author and David Higham Associates Ltd for 'The Force' by Peter Redgrove from *The Moon Disposes* (Secker and Warburg); Oxford University Press for 'North Wind: Portrush' from *The Hunt by Night* by Derek Mahon; J. C. Hall and Oxford University Press for 'Time Eating' by Keith Douglas from *The Complete Poems of Keith Douglas* edited by Desmond Graham (1978); Alison Young for 'On the Pilgrim's Road' and 'Wiltshire Downs' by Andrew Young; Chatto & Windus for 'Fetching Cows' by Norman MacCaig from *The Collected Poems of Norman MacCaig*; and the authors for 'Another September' by Thomas Kinsella and 'Privet' by Christopher Pilling.

Whilst every effort has been made to trace all copyright holders, the publishers apologise to any holders not acknowledged, and would be grateful to be notified of any corrections to be incorporated in future editions.

PLACES

Examine this region
Of short distances and definite places

W. H. Auden, 'In Praise of Limestone'

A writer is often someone who puts a particular region on the map, literally and figuratively, so that it becomes a mental possession as well as a physical one – Hardy's Wessex, Wordsworth's Lakes, Brontë Country, Dickens's London, Lawrence's Midlands, Scott's Border Country. And we all have a special feeling for our own neck of the woods, whether it has inspired poets or not:

Breathes there the man, with soul so dead,
Who never to himself hath said,
This is my own, my native land!

Walter Scott, 'Lay of the Last Minstrel'

We might not put it so grandly nowadays but the sentiment is universal and works as well for hamlets, villages, towns, counties and regions as it does for a whole country.

In this opening section I have travelled round Britain with the poets as they record and celebrate particular places, beginning with Lepe Beach in sight of the Isle of Wight and ending up in the remote Scottish islands. There is a twofold process going on in many of these poems, domestication and defamiliarisation, civilising the unknown and 'making strange' the known.

NEW YEAR'S DAY AT LEPE

Set out on a morning of white thaw
smoking between oaks, Hatchet Pond so still
it might have been frozen
except for the long slender rods
as if painted on its dark blue glaze.
Saw nothing of the *Private, Keep Out*
notices of semi-feudal estates,
but cock pheasants in brown fields
of sharp-edged clods, poking out their necks.
Then the small rusty bell of the shingle
tinkled and grated as it dragged,
a shadowy tanker bared its round stern
and Marchwood power station exhaled
a breath which the sun tinged pink;
but of all things none seemed newer
than gravel with its sheen of fresh oranges
at the water's lip. Brought away that,
and an old transparent moon
over the Island, the delicate industrial sky
blue-grey as a herring gull's back,
and a small sunny boy running beside
the great wet novelty shouting, *wasser, wasser.*

Jeremy Hooker (1941–)

ON THE PILGRIMS' ROAD

That I had hit the Road
  I partly knew
From a great Roman snail
  And sombre yew;
But that my steps went from
  And not towards
The shrine of good St Thomas,
  I thought of afterwards.

So I adored today
  No, not his ghost,
But the saints in Westwell window,
  And her the most
Who knelt there with no head
  But was so very
Adorable a saint
  In dress of crushed strawberry.

Andrew Young (1885–1971)

DOVER BEACH

The sea is calm to-night.
The tide is full, the moon lies fair
Upon the straits; – on the French coast the light
Gleams and is gone; the cliffs of England stand,
Glimmering and vast, out in the tranquil bay.
Come to the window, sweet is the night-air!
Only, from the long line of spray
Where the sea meets the moon-blanch'd land,
Listen! you hear the grating roar
Of pebbles which the waves draw back, and fling,

At their return, up the high strand,
Begin, and cease, and then again begin,
With tremulous cadence slow, and bring
The eternal note of sadness in.

Sophocles long ago
Heard it on the Ægæan, and it brought
Into his mind the turbid ebb and flow
Of human misery; we
Find also in the sound a thought,
Hearing it by this distant northern sea.

The sea of faith
Was once, too, at the full, and round earth's shore
Lay like the folds of a bright girdle furl'd.
But now I only hear
Its melancholy, long, withdrawing roar,
Retreating, to the breath
Of the night-wind, down the vast edges drear
And naked shingles of the world.

Ah, love, let us be true
To one another! for the world, which seems
To lie before us like a land of dreams,
So various, so beautiful, so new,
Hath really neither joy, nor love, nor light,
Nor certitude, nor peace, nor help for pain;
And we are here as on a darkling plain
Swept with confused alarms of struggle and flight,
Where ignorant armies clash by night.

Matthew Arnold (1822–1888)

DRIVING WEST

New car. One of the great
Roads of the west country
That Fielding remembered,
Dying abroad. Early

Winter morning with sun.
They make me feel sane and rich,
An eighteenth-century
Monseigneur in his coach

Who when the sparrows hopped
Down to his warm wheels, sure-
Winged but vulnerable,
Suddenly thought of the poor

And when a smiling dog
Trotted across the road,
Sharp-toothed but crushable,
For once pitied the mad.

Patricia Beer (1919–)

THIS LIME-TREE BOWER MY PRISON

[Addressed to Charles Lamb, of The India House, London]

In the June of 1797 some long-expected friends paid a visit to the author's cottage; and on the morning of their arrival, he met with an accident, which disabled him from walking during the whole time of their stay. One evening, when they had left him for a few hours, he composed the following lines in the garden-bower.

Well, they are gone, and here must I remain,
This lime-tree bower my prison! I have lost
Beauties and feelings, such as would have been
Most sweet to my remembrance even when age
Had dimm'd mine eyes to blindness! They, meanwhile,
Friends, whom I never more may meet again,
On springy heath, along the hill-top edge
Wander in gladness, and wind down, perchance,
To that still roaring dell, of which I told;
The roaring dell, o'erwooded, narrow, deep,
And only speckled by the mid-day sun;
Where its slim trunk the ash from rock to rock
Flings arching like a bridge; – that branchless ash,
Unsunn'd and damp, whose few poor yellow leaves
Ne'er tremble in the gale, yet tremble still,
Fann'd by the water-fall! and there my friends
Behold the dark green file of long lank weeds,
That all at once (a most fantastic sight!)
Still nod and drip beneath the dripping edge
Of the blue clay-stone.

                    Now, my friends emerge
Beneath the wide wide Heaven – and view again
The many-steepled tract magnificent
Of hilly fields and meadows, and the sea,
With some fair bark, perhaps, whose sails light up
The slip of smooth clear blue betwixt two Isles
Of purple shadow! Yes! they wander on

In gladness all; but thou, methinks, most glad,
My gentle-hearted Charles! for thou hast pined
And hunger'd after Nature, many a year,
In the great City pent, winning thy way
With sad yet patient soul, through evil and pain
And strange calamity! Ah! slowly sink
Behind the western ridge, thou glorious Sun!
Shine in the slant beams of the sinking orb,
Ye purple heath-flowers! richlier burn, ye clouds!
Live in the yellow light, ye distant groves!
And kindle, thou blue Ocean! so my friend
Struck with deep joy may stand, as I have stood,
Silent with swimming sense; yea, gazing round
On the wide landscape, gaze till all doth seem
Less gross than bodily; and of such hues
As veil the Almighty Spirit, when yet he makes
Spirits perceive his presence.

                                    A delight
Comes sudden on my heart, and I am glad
As I myself were there! Nor in this bower,
This little lime-tree bower, have I not mark'd
Much that has sooth'd me. Pale beneath the blaze
Hung the transparent foliage; and I watch'd
Some broad and sunny leaf, and lov'd to see
The shadow of the leaf and stem above
Dappling its sunshine! And that walnut-tree
Was richly ting'd, and a deep radiance lay
Full on the ancient ivy, which usurps
Those fronting elms, and now, with blackest mass
Makes their dark branches gleam a lighter hue
Through the late twilight: and though now the bat
Wheels silent by, and not a swallow twitters,
Yet still the solitary humble-bee
Sings in the bean-flower! Henceforth I shall know
That Nature ne'er deserts the wise and pure;

No plot so narrow, be but Nature there,
No waste so vacant, but may well employ
Each faculty of sense, and keep the heart
Awake to Love and Beauty! and sometimes
'Tis well to be bereft of promis'd good,
That we may lift the soul, and contemplate
With lively joy the joys we cannot share.
My gentle-hearted Charles! when the last rook
Beat its straight path along the dusky air
Homewards, I blest it! deeming its black wing
(Now a dim speck, now vanishing in light)
Had cross'd the mighty Orb's dilated glory,
While thou stood'st gazing; or, when all was still,
Flew creeking o'er thy head, and had a charm
For thee, my gentle-hearted Charles, to whom
No sound is dissonant which tells of Life.

S. T. Coleridge (1772–1834)

CORNISH WIND

There is a wind in Cornwall that I know
From any other wind, because it smells
Of the warm honey breath of heather-bells
And of the sea's salt; and these meet and flow
With such sweet savour in such sharpness met
That the astonished sense in ecstasy
Tastes the ripe earth and the unvintaged sea.
Wind out of Cornwall, wind, if I forget:
Not in the tunnelled streets where scarce men breathe
The air they live by, but whatever seas
Blossom in foam, wherever merchant bees
Volubly traffic upon any heath:
If I forget, shame me! or if I find
A wind in England like my Cornish wind.

Arthur Symons (1865–1945)

WILTSHIRE DOWNS

The cuckoo's double note
Loosened like bubbles from a drowning throat
Floats through the air
In mockery of pipit, lark and stare.

The stable-boys thud by
Their horses slinging divots at the sky
And with bright hooves
Printing the sodden turf with lucky grooves.

As still as a windhover
A shepherd in his flapping coat leans over
His tall sheep-crook
And shearlings, tegs and yoes cons like a book.

And one tree-crowned long barrow
Stretched like a sow that has brought forth her farrow
Hides a King's bones
Lying like broken sticks among the stones.

Andrew Young (1885–1971)

from ON WESTWELL DOWNS

When Westwell Downs I 'gan to tread,
Where cleanly winds the green did sweep,
Methought a landscape there was spread,
Here a bush and there a sheep:
    The pleated wrinkles of the face
    Of wave-swoln earth did lend such grace,
    As shadowings in Imag'ry
    Which both deceive and please the eye.

Here and there two hilly crests
Amidst them hug a pleasant green,
And these are like two swelling breasts
That close a tender fall between.
    Here would I sleep or read or pray
    From early morn till flight of day:
    But hark! a sheep-bell calls me up,
    Like Oxford college bells, to sup.

William Strode (1600–1645)

from THE PRELUDE

Book Thirteen

In one of these excursions, travelling then
Through Wales on foot, and with a youthful Friend,
I left Bethgelert's huts at couching-time,
And westward took my way to see the sun
Rise from the top of Snowdon. Having reach'd
The Cottage at the Mountain's foot, we there
Rouz'd up the Shepherd, who by ancient right
Of office is the Stranger's usual guide;
And after short refreshment sallied forth.

It was a Summer's night, a close warm night,
Wan, dull and glaring, with a dripping mist
Low-hung and thick that cover'd all the sky,
Half threatening storm and rain; but on we went
Uncheck'd, being full of heart and having faith
In our tried Pilot. Little could we see
Hemm'd round on every side with fog and damp,
And, after ordinary traveller's chat
With our Conductor, silently we sank
Each into commerce with his private thoughts:
Thus did we breast the ascent, and by myself
Was nothing either seen or heard the while
Which took me from my musings, save that once
The Shepherd's Cur did to his own great joy
Unearth a hedgehog in the mountain crags
Round which he made a barking turbulent.
This small adventure, for even such it seemed
In that wild place and at the dead of night,
Being over and forgotten, on we wound
In silence as before. With forehead bent
Earthward, as if in opposition set
Against an enemy, I panted up

With eager pace, and no less eager thoughts.
Thus might we wear perhaps an hour away,
Ascending at loose distance each from each,
And I, as chanced, the foremost of the Band:
When at my feet the ground appear'd to brighten,
And with a step or two seem'd brighter still;
Nor had I time to ask the cause of this,
For instantly a Light upon the turf
Fell like a flash: I looked about, and lo!
The Moon stood naked in the Heavens, at height
Immense above my head, and on the shore
I found myself of a huge sea of mist,
Which, meek and silent, rested at my feet:
A hundred hills their dusky backs upheaved
All over this still Ocean, and beyond,
Far, far beyond, the vapours shot themselves,
In headlands, tongues, and promontory shapes,
Into the Sea, the real Sea, that seem'd
To dwindle, and give up its majesty,
Usurp'd upon as far as sight could reach.
Meanwhile, the Moon look'd down upon this shew
In single glory, and we stood, the mist
Touching our very feet; and from the shore
At distance not the third part of a mile
Was a blue chasm; a fracture in the vapour,
A deep and gloomy breathing-place through which
Mounted the roar of waters, torrents, streams
Innumerable, roaring with one voice.
The universal spectacle throughout
Was shaped for admiration and delight,
Grand in itself alone, but in that breach
Through which the homeless voice of waters rose,
That dark deep thoroughfare had Nature lodg'd
The Soul, the Imagination of the whole.

William Wordsworth (1770–1850)

THE LAKE ISLE OF INNISFREE

(Lough Gill, Sligo)

I will arise and go now, and go to Innisfree,
And a small cabin build there, of clay and wattles made:
Nine bean-rows will I have there, a hive for the honey-bee,
And live alone in the bee-loud glade.

And I shall have some peace there, for peace comes dropping slow,
Dropping from the veils of the morning to where the cricket sings;
There midnight's all a glimmer, and noon a purple glow,
And evening full of the linnet's wings.

I will arise and go now, for always night and day
I hear lake water lapping with low sounds by the shore;
While I stand on the roadway, or on the pavements grey,
I hear it in the deep heart's core.

W. B. Yeats (1865–1939)

NORTH WIND: PORTRUSH

I shall never forget the wind
On this benighted coast.
It works itself into the mind
Like the high keen of a lost
Lear-spirit in agony
Condemned for eternity

To wander cliff and cove
Without comfort, without love.
It whistles off the stars
And the existential, black
Face of the cosmic dark:
We crouch to roaring fires.

Yet there are mornings when,
Even in midwinter, sunlight
Flares, and a rare stillness
Lies upon roof and garden,
Each object eldritch-bright,
The sea scarred but at peace.

Then, from the ship we say
Is the lit town where we live
(Our whiskey-and-forecast world),
A smaller ship that sheltered
All night in the restless bay
Will weigh anchor and leave.

What did they think of us
During their brief sojourn?
A string of lights on the prom
Dancing mad in the storm –
Who lives in such a place?
And will they ever return?

But the shops open at nine
As they have always done,
The wrapped-up bourgeoisie
Hardened by wind and sea.
The newspapers are late
But the milk shines in its crate.

Everything swept so clean
By tempest, wind and rain!
Elated, you might believe
That this was the first day –
A false sense of reprieve,
For the climate is here to stay.

So best prepare for the worst
That chaos and old night
Can do to us. Were we not
Raised on such expectations,
Our hearts starred with frost
Through countless generations?

Elsewhere the olive grove,
Le déjeuner sur l'herbe,
Poppies and parasols,
Blue skies and mythic love.
Here only the stricken souls
No spring can unperturb.

Prospero and his people never
Came to these stormy parts:
Few do who have the choice.
Yet, blasting the subtler arts,
That weird, plaintive voice
Choirs now and for ever.

Derek Mahon (1941–)

A SHROPSHIRE LAD

XXXI

On Wenlock Edge the wood's in trouble;
  His forest fleece the Wrekin heaves;
The gale, it plies the saplings double,
  And thick on Severn snow the leaves.

'Twould blow like this through holt and hanger
  When Uricon the city stood:
'Tis the old wind in the old anger,
  But then it threshed another wood.

Then, 'twas before my time, the Roman
  At yonder heaving hill would stare:
The blood that warms an English yeoman,
  The thoughts that hurt him, they were there.

There, like the wind through woods in riot,
  Through him the gale of life blew high;
The tree of man was never quiet:
  Then 'twas the Roman, now 'tis I.

The gale, it plies the saplings double,
  It blows so hard, 'twill soon be gone:
To-day the Roman and his trouble
  Are ashes under Uricon.

A. E. Housman (1859–1936)

from THE LOVER'S JOURNEY

First o'er a barren heath beside the coast
Orlando rode, and joy began to boast.

'This neat low gorse,' said he, 'with golden bloom,
Delights each sense, is beauty, is perfume;
And this gay ling, with all its purple flowers.
A man at leisure might admire for hours:
This green-fringed cup-moss has a scarlet tip,
That yields to nothing but my Laura's lip;
And then how fine this herbage! men may say
A heath is barren; nothing is so gay;
Barren or bare to call such charming scene
Argues a mind possess'd by care and spleen.'

Onward he went, and fiercer grew the heat,
Dust rose in clouds before the horse's feet;
For now he pass'd through lanes of burning sand,
Bounds to thin crops or yet uncultured land;
Where the dark poppy flourish'd on the dry
And sterile soil, and mock'd the thin-set rye.

'How lovely this!' the rapt Orlando said;
'With what delight is labouring man repaid!
The very lane has sweets that all admire,
The rambling suckling, and the vigorous brier;
See! wholesome wormwood grows beside the way,
Where dew-press'd yet the dog-rose bends the spray;
Fresh herbs the fields, fair shrubs the banks adorn,
And snow-white bloom falls flaky from the thorn;
No fostering hand they need, no sheltering wall,
They spring uncultured, and they bloom for all.'

*   *   *

Beneath an ancient bridge, the straiten'd flood
Rolls through its sloping banks of slimy mud;
Near it a sunken boat resists the tide,
That frets and hurries to th' opposing side;
The rushes sharp, that on the borders grow,
Bend their brown flow'rets to the stream below,
Impure in all its course, in all its progress slow:
Here a grave Flora scarcely deigns to bloom,
Nor wears a rosy blush, nor sheds perfume;
The few dull flowers that o'er the place are spread
Partake the nature of their fenny bed;
Here on its wiry stem, in rigid bloom,
Grows the salt lavender that lacks perfume;
Here the dwarf sallows creep, the septfoil harsh,
And the soft slimy mallow of the marsh;
Low on the ear the distant billows sound,
And just in view appears their stony bound;
No hedge nor tree conceals the glowing sun,
Birds, save a wat'ry tribe, the district shun,
Nor chirp among the reeds where bitter waters run.

'Various as beauteous, Nature, is thy face,'
Exclaim'd Orlando: 'all that grows has grace;
All are appropriate – bog, and marsh, and fen,
Are only poor to undiscerning men;
Here may the nice and curious eye explore
How Nature's hand adorns the rushy moor;
Here the rare moss in secret shade is found,
Here the sweet myrtle of the shaking ground;
Beauties are these that from the view retire;
But well repay th' attention they require;
For these, my Laura will her home forsake,
And all the pleasures they afford partake.'

*   *   *

[*Orlando's mood changes abruptly when he finds that his Laura is not at home, but 'gone to see a friend'.*]

*   *   *

Forth rode Orlando by a river's side,
Inland and winding, smooth, and full and wide,
That roll'd majestic on, in one soft-flowing tide;
The bottom gravel, flow'ry were the banks,
Tall willows, waving in their broken ranks:
The road, now near, now distant, winding led
By lovely meadows which the waters fed;
He pass'd the way-side inn, the village spire,
Nor stopp'd to gaze, to question, or admire;
On either side the rural mansions stood,
With hedge-row trees, and hills high-crown'd with wood,
And many a devious stream that reach'd the noble flood.

'I hate these scenes,' Orlando angry cried,
'And these proud farmers! yes, I hate their pride:
See! that sleek fellow, how he strides along,
Strong as an ox, and ignorant as strong;
Can yon close crops a single eye detain
But he who counts the profits of the grain?
And these vile beans with deleterious smell,
Where is their beauty? can a mortal tell?
These deep fat meadows I detest; it shocks
One's feelings there to see the grazing ox; –
For slaughter fatted, as a lady's smile
Rejoices man, and means his death the while.
Lo! now the sons of labour! every day
Employ'd in toil, and vex'd in every way;
Theirs is but mirth assumed, and they conceal,
In their affected joys, the ills they feel:
I hate these long green lanes; there's nothing seen
In this vile country but eternal green;
Woods! waters! meadows! Will they never end?
'Tis a vile prospect: – Gone to see a friend!' –

George Crabbe (1754–1832)

38

WHY WRITE OF THE SUN

when all it has done for us this last year
is dawdle in rain water smeared on the windscreen
or glisten carelessly across drying flagstones.
Take the week of the cottage in Anglesey:
just one afternoon to speak of when we flopped

like synchronised seals into Red Wharf Bay.
Then the drizzle came, the swingball splattered
like a dishcloth and a bike ride to Moelfre
blackened our spines with a plume of dirt.
After three sticky nights we called it a day.

Take the camping weekend under Malham Cove:
drunk with the effort of filling the air-beds
we saw stars spangle in the one-man tent.
Then we slept with a thunderstorm drum-rolling
over us, and dreamt of everlasting happiness

as we drifted apart on the waterlogged groundsheet.
Take the walk along the Humber Bridge
with the wind nagging the high-tension cables.
All we had to time the distance to the waves
was a spent match, and you told me to drop it.

Admittedly, there was one evening; mackerel sky,
the laburnum apparently cascading with yellow
and a breath of air almost saying something
through the trellis. But why write of whispering
when all we ever did that year was shout.

Simon Armitage (1963–)

from EPISTLE TO CHARLES BRADSHAW, ESQ.

But being now cur'd of that malady,
I'm at full leisure to remember thee,
And (which I'm sure you long to know) set forth
In Northern song my journey to the North.

Know then with horses twain, one sound, one lame,
On Sunday's eve I to St Albans came,
Where, finding by my body's lusty state,
I could not hold out home at that slow rate,
I found a coachman, who, my case bemoaning,
With three stout geldings, and one able stoning,
For eight good pounds did bravely undertake,
Or for my own, or for my money's sake,
Through thick and thin, fall out what could befall,
To bring me safe and sound to Basford Hall.

Which having drunk upon, he bid good-night,
And (Heaven forgive us) with the morning's light,
Not fearing God, nor his vicegerent constable,
We roundly rowling were the road to Dunstable,
Which, as they chim'd to prayers, we trotted through,
And 'fore elev'n ten minutes came unto
The town that Brickhill hight, where we did rest,
And din'd indifferent well both man and beast.
'Twixt two and four to Stratford, 'twas well driven,
And came to Tocester to lodge at even.
Next day we din'd at Dunchurch, and did lie
That night four miles on our side Coventry.
Tuesday at noon at Lichfield town we baited,
But there some friends, who long that hour had waited,
So long detain'd me, that my charioteer
Could drive that night but to Uttoxeter.

And where the Wedn'sday, being market day,
I was constrain'd with some kind lads to stay
Tippling till afternoon, which made it night
When from my Hero's Tower I saw the light
Of her flambeaux, and fanci'd as we drave
Each rising hillock was a swelling wave,
And that I swimming was in Neptune's spight,
To my long long'd for harbour of delight.

And now I'm here set down again in peace,
After my troubles, business, voyages,
The same dull Northern clod I was before,
Gravely enquiring how ewes are a score,
How the hay harvest, and the corn was got,
And if or no there's like to be a rot;
Just the same sot I was e'er I remov'd;
Nor by my travel, nor the Court improv'd;
The same old-fashion'd Squire, no whit refin'd,
And shall be wiser when the Devil's blind . . .

Charles Cotton (1630–1687)

stoning stallion

WUTHERING HEIGHTS

The horizons ring me like faggots,
Tilted and disparate, and always unstable.
Touched by a match, they might warm me,
And their fine lines singe
The air to orange
Before the distances they pin evaporate,
Weighting the pale sky with a solider colour.
But they only dissolve and dissolve
Like a series of promises, as I step forward.

There is no life higher than the grasstops
Or the hearts of sheep, and the wind
Pours by like destiny, bending
Everything in one direction.
I can feel it trying
To funnel my heat away.
If I pay the roots of the heather
Too close attention, they will invite me
To whiten my bones among them.

The sheep know where they are,
Browsing in their dirty wool-clouds,
Grey as the weather.
The black slots of their pupils take me in.
It is like being mailed into space,
A thin, silly message.
They stand about in grandmotherly disguise,
All wig curls and yellow teeth
And hard, marbly baas.

I come to wheel ruts, and water
Limpid as the solitudes
That flee through my fingers.
Hollow doorsteps go from grass to grass;
Lintel and sill have unhinged themselves.
Of people the air only
Remembers a few odd syllables.
It rehearses them moaningly:
Black stone, black stone.

The sky leans on me, me, the one upright
Among all horizontals.
The grass is beating its head distractedly.
It is too delicate
For a life in such company;
Darkness terrifies it.
Now, in valleys narrow
And black as purses, the house lights
Gleam like small change.

Sylvia Plath (1932–1962)

43

from ELEGIAC STANZAS

*Suggested by a Picture of Peele Castle in a Storm,
painted by Sir George Beaumont*

I was thy neighbour once, thou rugged Pile!
    Four summer weeks I dwelt in sight of thee:
I saw thee every day; and all the while
    Thy form was sleeping on a glassy sea.

So pure the sky, so quiet was the air!
    So like, so very like, was day to day!
Whene'er I look'd, thy image still was there;
    It trembled, but it never pass'd away.

How perfect was the calm! It seem'd no sleep,
    No mood, which season takes away, or brings:
I could have fancied that the mighty Deep
    Was even the gentlest of all gentle things.

Ah! then if mine had been the Painter's hand
    To express what then I saw; and add the gleam,
The light that never was on sea or land,
    The consecration, and the Poet's dream, –

William Wordsworth (1770–1850)

FROM A BOAT AT CONISTON

I look into the lake (the lacquered water
Black with the sunset), watching my own face.
Tiny red-ribbed fishes swim
In and out of the nostrils, long-tongued weeds
Lick at the light that oozes down from the surface,
And bubbles rise from the eyes like aerated
Tears shed there in the element of mirrors.
My sight lengthens its focus; sees the sky
Laid level upon the glass, the loud
World of the wind and the map-making clouds and history
Squinting over the rim of the fell. The wind
lets on the water, paddling like a duck,
And face and cloud are grimaced out
In inch-deep wrinkles of the moving waves.
A blackbird clatters; alder leaves
Make mooring buoys for the water beetles.
I wait for the wind to drop, against hope
Hoping, and against the weather, yet to see
The water empty, the water full of itself,
Free of the sky and the cloud and free of me.

Norman Nicholson (1914–1987)

ROMAN WALL BLUES

Over the heather the wet wind blows,
I've lice in my tunic and a cold in my nose.

The rain comes pattering out of the sky,
I'm a Wall soldier, I don't know why.

The mist creeps over the hard grey stone,
My girl's in Tungria; I sleep alone.

Aulus goes hanging around her place,
I don't like his manners, I don't like his face.

Piso's a Christian, he worships a fish;
There'd be no kissing if he had his wish.

She gave me a ring but I diced it away;
I want my girl and I want my pay.

When I'm a veteran with only one eye
I shall do nothing but look at the sky.

W. H. Auden (1907–1973)

INVERSNAID

This darksome burn, horseback brown,
His rollrock highroad roaring down,
In coop and in comb the fleece of his foam
Flutes and low to the lake falls home.

A windpuff-bonnet of fawn-froth
Turns and twindles over the broth
Of a pool so pitchblack, fell-frowning,
It rounds and rounds Despair to drowning.

Degged with dew, dappled with dew
Are the groins of the braes that the brook treads through,
Wiry hearthpacks, flitches of fern,
And the beadbonny ash that sits over the burn.

What would the world be, once bereft
Of wet and of wildness? Let them be left,
O let them be left, wildness and wet;
Long live the weeds and the wilderness yet.

Gerard Manley Hopkins (1844–1889)

from THE BOTHIE OF TOBER-NA-VUOLICH

III

NAMQUE CANEBAT UTI

There is a stream, I name not its name, lest inquisitive tourist
Hunt it, and make it a lion, and get it at last into guide-books,
Springing far off from a loch unexplored in the folds of great
      mountains,
Falling two miles through rowan and stunted alder, enveloped
Then for four more in a forest of pine, where broad and ample
Spreads, to convey it, the glen with heathery slopes on both sides:
Broad and fair the stream, with occasional falls and narrows;
But, where the glen of its course approaches the vale of the river,
Met and blocked by a huge interposing mass of granite,
Scarce by a channel deep-cut, raging up, and raging onward,
Forces its flood through a passage so narrow a lady would step it.
There, across the great rocky wharves, a wooden bridge goes,
Carrying a path to the forest; below, three hundred yards, say,
Lower in level some twenty-five feet, through flats of shingle,
Stepping-stones and a cart-track cross in the open valley.
    But in the interval here the boiling, pent-up water
Frees itself by a final descent, attaining a bason,
Ten feet wide and eighteen long, with whiteness and fury
Occupied partly, but mostly pellucid, pure, a mirror;
Beautiful there for the colour derived from green rocks under;
Beautiful, most of all, where beads of foam uprising
Mingle their clouds of white with the delicate hue of the stillness.
Cliff over cliff for its sides, with rowan and pendent birch boughs,
Here it lies, unthought of above at the bridge and pathway,
Still more enclosed from below by wood and rocky projection.
You are shut in, left alone with yourself and perfection of water,
Hid on all sides, left alone with yourself and the goddess of bathing.

*   *   *

For it was told, the Piper narrating, corrected of Arthur,
Often by word corrected, more often by smile and motion,
How they had been to Iona, to Staffa, to Skye, to Culloden,
Seen Loch Awe, Loch Tay, Loch Fyne, Loch Ness, Loch Arkaig,
Been up Ben-nevis, Ben-more, Ben-cruachan, Ben-muick-dhui;
How they had walked, and eaten, and drunken, and slept in
    kitchens,
Slept upon floors of kitchens, and tasted the real Glen-livat,
Walked up perpendicular hills, and also down them,
Hither and thither had been, and this and that had witnessed,
Left not a thing to be done, and had not a copper remaining.
    For it was told withal, he telling, and he correcting,
How in the race they had run, and beaten the gillies of Rannoch,
How in forbidden glens, in Mar and midmost Athol,
Philip insisting hotly, and Arthur and Hope compliant,
They had defied the keepers; the Piper alone protesting,
Liking the fun, it was plain, in his heart, but tender of game-law;
Yea, too, in Meäly glen, the heart of Lochiel's fair forest,
Where Scotch firs are darkest and amplest, and intermingle
Grandly with rowan and ash – in Mar you have no ashes,
There the pine is alone, or relieved by the birch and the alder –
How in Meäly glen, while stags were starting before, they
Made the watcher believe they were guests from Achnacarry.

Arthur Hugh Clough (1819–1861)

49

BY FERRY TO THE ISLAND

We crossed by ferry to the bare island
where sheep and cows stared coldly through the wind –
the sea behind us with its silver water,
the silent ferryman standing in the stern
clutching his coat about him like old iron.

We landed from the ferry and went inland
past a small church down to the winding shore
where a white seagull fallen from the failing
chill and ancient daylight lay so pure
and softly breasted that it made more dear

the lesser white around us. There we sat
sheltered by a rock beside the sea.
Someone made coffee, someone played the fool
in a high rising voice for two hours.
The sea's language was more grave and harsh.

And one sat there whose dress was white and cool.
The fool sparkled his wit that she might hear
new diamonds turning on her naked finger.
What might the sea think or the dull sheep
lifting its head through heavy Sunday sleep?

And later, going home, a moon rising
at the end of a cart-track, minimum of red,
the wind being dark, imperfect cows staring
out of their half-intelligence, and a plough
lying on its side in the cold, raw

naked twilight, there began to move
slowly, like heavy water, in the heart
the image of the gull and of that dress,
both being white and out of the darkness rising
the moon ahead of us with its rusty ring.

Iain Crichton Smith (1928–)

from ON A RAISED BEACH

To James H. Whyte

Deep conviction or preference can seldom
Find direct terms in which to express itself.
Today on this shingle shelf
I understand this pensive reluctance so well,
This not discommendable obstinacy,
These contrivances of an inexpressive critical feeling,
These stones with their resolve that Creation shall not be
Injured by iconoclasts and quacks. Nothing has stirred
Since I lay down this morning an eternity ago
But one bird. The widest open door is the least liable to intrusion,
Ubiquitous as the sunlight, unfrequented as the sun.
The inward gates of a bird are always open.
It does not know how to shut them.
That is the secret of its song,
But whether any man's are ajar is doubtful.
I look at these stones and know little about them,
But I know their gates are open too,
Always open, far longer open, than any bird's can be,
That every one of them has had its gates wide open far longer
Than all birds put together, let alone humanity,
Though through them no man can see,
No man nor anything more recently born than themselves
And that is everything else on the Earth.
I too lying here have dismissed all else.
Bread from stones is my sole and desperate dearth,
From stones, which are to the Earth as to the sunlight
Is the naked sun which is for no man's sight.
I would scorn to cry to any easier audience
Or, having cried, to lack patience to await the response.
I am no more indifferent or ill-disposed to life than death is:
I would fain accept it all completely as the soil does;
Already I feel all that can perish perishing in me

As so much has perished and all will yet perish in these stones.
I must begin with these stones as the world began.

       *   *   *

This is no heap of broken images.
Let me find the faith that builds mountains
Before they seek the faith that moves them. Men cannot hope
To survive the fall of the mountains
Which they will no more see than they saw their rise
Unless they are more concentrated and determined,
Truer to themselves and with more to be true to,
Than those stones, and as inerrable as they are.
Their sole concern is that what can be shaken
Shall be shaken and disappear
And only the unshakable be left.
What hardihood in any man has part or parcel in the latter?
It is necessary to make a stand and maintain it forever.
These stones go through Man, straight to God, if there is one.
What have they not gone through already?
Empires, civilisations, aeons. Only in them
If in anything, can His creation confront Him.
They came so far out of the water and halted forever.
That larking dallier, the sun, has only been able to play
With superficial by-products since;
The moon moves the waters backwards and forwards,
But the stones cannot be lured an inch farther
Either on this side of eternity or the other.
Who thinks God is easier to know than they are?
Trying to reach men any more, any otherwise, than they are?
These stones will reach us long before we reach them.
Cold, undistracted, eternal and sublime.
They will stem all the torrents of vicissitude forever
With a more than Roman peace.

Hugh MacDiarmid (1892–1978)

FISH, FLESH OR FOWL

Fish, flesh or fowl, commend all summer long
Whatever is begotten, born, and dies

W. B. Yeats, 'Sailing to Byzantium'

Poetry celebrates all those other life-forms we share the planet with, from Keats's gnats in 'Ode to Autumn' to the cows Norman MacCaig brings home from pasture.

We celebrate them for their own sake and as a means of further understanding ourselves, as in Blake's 'Tyger', Hopkins's 'Windhover' and Hughes's 'Wodwo' (a mythical wood spirit taken from medieval literature). The bird as emblem of the free soul, animals as emblems of all the virtues and vices, are found everywhere in world literature, and on flags and coats of arms – and are brought to us in close-up on television nowadays, complete with a voice-over storyline. They are Keats's 'poetry of earth' itself, which crawls, swims, bounds and swoops through our waking and sleeping lives.

Blake and Lawrence were anxious that we should recognise and respect the 'otherness' of animal creation, and not use it merely as a peg on which to hang our own selfish preoccupations. In modern times the indiscriminate slaughter of wildlife has finally made us question our Biblical 'dominion . . . over every living thing'.

THE WILD SWANS AT COOLE

(Coole Park, Galway)

The trees are in their autumn beauty,
The woodland paths are dry,
Under the October twilight the water
Mirrors a still sky;
Upon the brimming water among the stones
Are nine-and-fifty swans.

The nineteenth autumn has come upon me
Since I first made my count;
I saw, before I had well finished,
All suddenly mount
And scatter wheeling in great broken rings
Upon their clamorous wings.

I have looked upon those brilliant creatures,
And now my heart is sore.
All's changed since I, hearing at twilight,
The first time on this shore,
The bell-beat of their wings above my head,
Trod with a lighter tread.

Unwearied still, lover by lover,
They paddle in the cold
Companionable streams or climb the air;
Their hearts have not grown old;
Passion or conquest, wander where they will,
Attend upon them still.

But now they drift on the still water,
Mysterious, beautiful;
Among what rushes will they build,
By what lake's edge or pool
Delight men's eyes when I awake some day
To find they have flown away?

W. B. Yeats (1865–1939)

from DUCKS

I

From troubles of the world
I turn to ducks,
Beautiful comical things
Sleeping or curled
Their heads beneath white wings
By water cool,
Or finding curious things
To eat in various mucks
Beneath the pool,
Tails uppermost, or waddling
Sailor-like on the shores
Of ponds, or paddling
– Left! right! – with fanlike feet
Which are for steady oars
When they (white galleys) float
Each bird a boat
Rippling at will the sweet
Wide waterway . . .
When night is fallen *you* creep
Upstairs, but drakes and dillies
Nest with pale water-stars,
Moonbeams and shadow bars,
And water-lilies:
Fearful too much to sleep
Since they've no locks
To click against the teeth
Of weasel and fox.
And warm beneath
Are eggs of cloudy green
Whence hungry rats and lean
Would stealthily suck
New life, but for the mien,

The bold ferocious mien
Of the mother-duck.

II

Yes, ducks are valiant things
On nests of twigs and straws,
And ducks are soothy things
And lovely on the lake
When that the sunlight draws
Thereon their picture dim
In colours cool.
And when beneath the pool
They dabble, and when they swim
And make their rippling rings,
O ducks are beautiful things!

But ducks are comical things: –
As comical as you.
Quack!
They waddle round, they do.
They eat all sorts of things,
And then they quack.
By barn and stable and stack
They wander at their will,
But if you go too near
They look at you through black
Small topaz-tinted eyes
And wish you ill.
Triangular and clear
They leave their curious track
In mud at the water's edge,
And there amid the sedge
And slime they gobble and peer
Saying 'Quack! quack!'

F. W. Harvey (1888–1957)

ON SEEING A PIGEON MAKE LOVE

Is not the picture strangely like?
Doesn't the very bowing strike?
Can any art of love in fashion
Express a more prevailing passion?
That air – that sticking to her side –
That deference, ill-concealing pride, –
That seeming consciousness of coat,
And repetition of one note, –
Ducking and tossing back his head,
As if at every bow he said,
'Madam, by God', – or 'Strike me dead'.

And then the lady! look at her:
What bridling sense of character!
How she declines, and seems to go,
Yet still endures him to and fro;
Carrying her plumes and pretty clothings,
Blushing stare, and muttered nothings,
Body plump, and airy feet,
Like any charmer in a street.

Give him a hat beneath his wing,
And is not he the very thing?
Give her a parasol or plaything,
And is not she the very she-thing?

James Leigh Hunt (1784–1859)

THE TWA CORBIES

As I was walking all alane,
I heard twa corbies making a mane;
The tane unto the t'other say,
'Where sall we gang and dine to-day?'

'In behint yon auld fail dyke,
I wot their lies a new-slain knight;
And nae body kens that he lies there,
But his hawk, his hound, and lady fair.

'His hound is to the hunting gane,
His hawk to fetch the wild-fowl hame,
His lady's ta'en another mate,
So we may make our dinner sweet.

'Ye'll sit on his white hause bane,
And I'll pike out his bonny blue een:
Wi' ae lock o' his gowden hair,
We'll theek our nest when it grows bare.

'Mony a one for him makes mane,
But nane sall ken whare he is gane:
O'er his white banes, when they are bare,
The wind sall blaw for evermair.'

Anon (16th Century?)

corbies crows *fail dyke* turf wall *hause* neck *theek* thatch

OWL

is my favourite. Who flies
like a nothing through the night,
who-whoing. Is a feather
duster in leafy corners ring-a-rosy-ing
boles of mice. Twice

you hear him call. Who
is he looking for? You hear
him hoovering over the floor
of the wood. O would you be gold
rings in the driving skull

if you could? Hooded and
vulnerable by the winter suns
owl looks. Is the grain of bark
in the dark. Round beaks are at
work in the pellety nest,

resting. Owl is an eye
in the barn. For a hole
in the trunk owl's blood
is to blame. Black talons in the
petrified fur! Cold walnut hands

on the case of the brain! In the reign
of the chicken owl comes like
a god. Is a goad in
the rain to the pink eyes,
dripping. For a meal in the day

flew, killed, on the moor. Six
mouths are the seed of his
arc in the season. Torn meat
from the sky. Owl lives
by the claws of his brain. On the branch

in the sever of the hand's
twigs owl is a backward look.
Flown wind in the skin. Fine
rain in the bones. Owl breaks
like the day. Am an owl, am an owl.

George Macbeth (1932–1992)

THE DARKLING THRUSH

I leant upon a coppice gate
    When Frost was spectre-gray,
And Winter's dregs made desolate
    The weakening eye of day.
The tangled bine-stems scored the sky
    Like strings of broken lyres,
And all mankind that haunted nigh
    Had sought their household fires.

The land's sharp features seemed to be
    The Century's corpse outleant,
His crypt the cloudy canopy,
    The wind his death-lament.
The ancient pulse of germ and birth
    Was shrunken hard and dry,
And every spirit upon earth
    Seemed fervourless as I.

At once a voice arose among
    The bleak twigs overhead
In a full-hearted evensong
    Of joy illimited;
An agèd thrush, frail, gaunt, and small,
    In blast-beruffled plume,
Had chosen thus to fling his soul
    Upon the growing gloom.

So little cause for carolings
    Of such ecstatic sound
Was written on terrestrial things
    Afar or nigh around,
That I could think there trembled through
    His happy good-night air
Some blessèd Hope, whereof he knew
    And I was unaware.

31 December 1900

Thomas Hardy (1840–1928)

AFTER DEATH

Opening up the house
After three weeks away
I found bird droppings
All over the ground floor,
White and heavy on the windows,
On the worktop,
On the cupboards,
On every wild hope of freedom.

I could not find any bird
At first, and feared
Some science fiction mystery,
To be horribly explained
As soon as whatever
It was felt sure
It had got me alone,
A mile from the village.

At last I discovered him,
Weightless and out of the running,
More null than old wrapping paper
A month after Christmas.
No food inside him, of course,
He had died of hunger
And no waste either,
He was quite empty.

His desperate ghost
Flew down my throat and my ears.
There was no air
He had not suffered in.
He lay in one place,
His droppings were everywhere
More vivid, more terrible
Than he had been, ever.

Patricia Beer (1919–)

ON THE GRASSHOPPER AND CRICKET

The poetry of earth is never dead:
   When all the birds are faint with the hot sun,
   And hide in cooling trees, a voice will run
From hedge to hedge about the new-mown mead –
That is the Grasshopper's. He takes the lead
   In summer luxury; he has never done
   With his delights, for when tired out with fun
He rests at ease beneath some pleasant weed.
The poetry of earth is ceasing never:
   On a lone winter evening, when the frost
     Has wrought a silence, from the stove there shrills
The Cricket's song, in warmth increasing ever,
   And seems to one in drowsiness half lost,
     The Grasshopper's among some grassy hills.

John Keats (1795–1821)

MOUSE'S NEST

I found a ball of grass among the hay
And progged it as I passed and went away;
And when I looked I fancied something stirred,
And turned agen and hoped to catch the bird –
When out an old mouse bolted in the wheats
With all her young ones hanging at her teats;
She looked so odd and so grotesque to me,
I ran and wondered what the thing could be,
And pushed the knapweed bunches where I stood;
Then the mouse hurried from the craking brood,
The young ones squeaked, and as I went away
She found her nest again among the hay.
The water o'er the pebbles scarce could run
And broad old cesspools glittered in the sun.

John Clare (1793–1864)

FETCHING COWS

The black one, last as usual, swings her head
And coils a black tongue round a grass-tuft. I
Watch her soft weight come down, her split feet spread.

In front, the others swing and slouch; they roll
Their Greek eyes and breathe out milky gusts
From muzzles black and shiny as wet coal.

The collie trots, bored, at my heels, then plops
Into the ditch. The sea makes a tired sound
That's always stopping though it never stops.

A haycart squats prickeared against the sky.
Hay breath and milk breath. Far out in the West
The wrecked sun founders though its colours fly.

The collie's bored. There's nothing to control . . .
The black cow is two native carriers
Bringing its belly home, slung from a pole.

Norman MacCaig (1910–)

A SHEEP FAIR

The day arrives of the autumn fair,
          And torrents fall,
Though sheep in throngs are gathered there,
          Ten thousand all,
Sodden, with hurdles round them reared:
And lot by lot, the pens are cleared,
And the auctioneer wrings out his beard,
And wipes his book, bedrenched and smeared,
And rakes the rain from his face with the edge of his hand,
          As torrents fall.

The wool of the ewes is like a sponge
          With the daylong rain:
Jammed tight, to turn, or lie, or lunge,
          They strive in vain.
Their horns are soft as finger-nails,
Their shepherds reek against the rails,
The tied dogs soak with tucked-in tails,
The buyers' hat-brims fill like pails,
Which spill small cascades when they shift their stand
          In the daylong rain.

POSTSCRIPT

Time has trailed lengthily since met
          At Pummery Fair
Those panting thousands in their wet
          And woolly wear:
And every flock long since has bled,
And all the dripping buyers have sped,
And the hoarse auctioneer is dead,
Who 'Going – going!' so often said,
As he consigned to doom each meek, mewed band
          At Pummery Fair.

Thomas Hardy (1840–1928)

TO HIS WIFE, FOR STRIKING HER DOG

Your little dog, that barked as I came by,
I strake by hap so hard I made him cry;
And straight you put your finger in your eye,
And louring sat. I asked the reason why.
'Love me, and love my dog,' thou didst reply.
'Love as both should be loved.' – 'I will,' said I,
And sealed it with a kiss. Then by and by,
Cleared were the clouds of thy fair frowning sky.
Thus small events, greater masteries may try.
 For I, by this, do at their meaning guess,
 That beat a whelp afore a lioness.

Sir John Harington (1561–1612)

EPIGRAM
ENGRAVED ON THE COLLAR OF A DOG
WHICH I GAVE TO HIS ROYAL HIGHNESS

I am his Highness' Dog at *Kew*;
Pray tell me Sir, whose Dog are you?

Alexander Pope (1688–1744)

from **BADGER**

When midnight comes a host of dogs and men
Go out and track the badger to his den,
And put a sack within the hole, and lie
Till the old grunting badger passes by.
He comes and hears – they let the strongest loose.
The old fox hears the noise and drops the goose.
The poacher shoots and hurries from the cry,
And the old hare half wounded buzzes by.
They get a forked stick to bear him down
And clap the dogs and take him to the town,
And bait him all the day with many dogs,
And laugh and shout and fright the scampering hogs.
He runs along and bites at all he meets:
They shout and hollo down the noisy streets.

He turns about to face the loud uproar
And drives the rebels to their very door.
The frequent stone is hurled where'er they go;
When badgers fight, then every one's a foe.
The dogs are clapt and urged to join the fray;
The badger turns and drives them all away.
Though scarcely half as big, demure and small,
He fights with dogs for hours and beats them all.
The heavy mastiff, savage in the fray,
Lies down and licks his feet and turns away.
The bulldog knows his match and waxes cold,
The badger grins and never leaves his hold.
He drives the crowd and follows at their heels
And bites them through – the drunkard swears and reels.

The frighted women take the boys away,
The blackguard laughs and hurries on the fray.
He tries to reach the woods, an awkward race,
But sticks and cudgels quickly stop the chase.
He turns agen and drives the noisy crowd
And beats the many dogs in noises loud.
He drives away and beats them every one,
And then they loose them all and set them on.
He falls as dead and kicked by boys and men,
Then starts and grins and drives the crowd agen;
Till kicked and torn and beaten out he lies
And leaves his hold and cackles, groans, and dies.

John Clare (1793–1864)

EPITAPH ON A HARE

Here lies, whom hound did ne'er pursue,
    Nor swifter greyhound follow,
Whose foot ne'er tainted morning dew,
    Nor ear heard huntsman's halloo,

Old Tiney, surliest of his kind,
    Who, nurs'd with tender care,
And to domestic bounds confin'd,
    Was still a wild Jack-hare.

Though duly from my hand he took
    His pittance ev'ry night,
He did it with a jealous look,
    And, when he could, would bite.

His diet was of wheaten bread,
    And milk, and oats, and straw;
Thistles, or lettuces instead,
    With sand to scour his maw.

On twigs of hawthorn he regal'd,
    On pippins' russet peel,
And, when his juicy salads fail'd,
    Slic'd carrot pleas'd him well.

A Turkey carpet was his lawn,
    Whereon he lov'd to bound,
To skip and gambol like a fawn,
    And swing his rump around.

His frisking was at ev'ning hours,
    For then he lost his fear,
But most before approaching show'rs,
    Or when a storm drew near.

Eight years and five round-rolling moons
    He thus saw steal away,
Dozing out all his idle noons,
    And ev'ry night at play.

I kept him for his humour's sake,
    For he would oft beguile
My heart of thoughts, that made it ache,
    And force me to a smile.

But now beneath his walnut shade
    He finds his long last home,
And waits in snug concealment laid,
    Till gentler Puss shall come.

He still more aged feels the shocks,
    From which no care can save,
And, partner once of Tiney's box,
    Must soon partake his grave.

William Cowper (1731–1800)

from VENUS AND ADONIS

WILD BOAR

'Thou hadst been gone,' quoth she, 'sweet boy, ere this,
But that thou told'st me, thou wouldst hunt the boar.
Oh be advis'd, thou know'st not what it is,
With javelin's point a churlish swine to gore,
      Whose tushes never sheath'd he whetteth still,
      Like to a mortal butcher, bent to kill.

'On his bow-back he hath a battle set
Of bristly pikes that ever threat his foes;
His eyes like glow-worms shine when he doth fret,
His snout digs sepulchres where'er he goes;
      Being mov'd, he strikes whate'er is in his way,
      And whom he strikes his crooked tushes slay.

'His brawny sides with hairy bristles armed
Are better proof than thy spear's point can enter;
His short thick neck cannot be easily harmed;
Being ireful, on the lion he will venture.
      The thorny brambles and embracing bushes,
      As fearful of him, part; through whom he rushes.

'Alas, he naught esteems that face of thine,
To which love's eyes pays tributary gazes;
Nor thy soft hands, sweet lips and crystal eyne,
Whose full perfection all the world amazes:
      But having thee at vantage – wondrous dread! –
      Would root these beauties as he roots the mead.'

William Shakespeare (1564–1616)

THE THOUGHT-FOX

I imagine this midnight moment's forest:
Something else is alive
Beside the clock's loneliness
And this blank page where my fingers move.

Through the window I see no star:
Something more near
Though deeper within darkness
Is entering the loneliness:

Cold, delicately as the dark snow,
A fox's nose touches twig, leaf;
Two eyes serve a movement, that now
And again now, and now, and now

Sets neat prints into the snow
Between trees, and warily a lame
Shadow lags by stump and in hollow
Of a body that is bold to come

Across clearings, an eye,
A widening deepening greeness,
Brilliantly, concentratedly,
Coming about its own business

Till, with a sudden sharp hot stink of fox
It enters the dark hole of the head.
The window is starless still; the clock ticks,
The page is printed.

Ted Hughes (1930–)

from **BRITANNIA'S PASTORALS**

SQUIRREL

Then as a nimble squirrel from the wood,
Ranging the hedges for his filbert food,
Sits pertly on a bough his brown nuts cracking,
And from the shell the sweet white kernel taking,
Till, with their crooks and bags, a sort of boys,
To share with him, come with so great a noise
That he is forced to leave a nut nigh broke,
And for his life leap to a neighbour oak;
Thence to a beech, thence to a row of ashes;
Whilst, through the quagmires and red water plashes,
The boys run dabbling through thick and thin,
One tears his hose, another breaks his shin;
This, torn and tattered, hath with much ado
Got by the briars; and that hath lost his shoe;
This drops his band; that headlong falls for haste;
Another cries behind for being last:
With sticks and stones and many a sounding hollo
The little fool, with no small sport, they follow,
Whilst he, from tree to tree, from spray to spray,
Gets to the wood and hides him in his dray:
Such shift made Ryot, ere he could get up,
And so from bough to bough he won the top.

William Browne (1591?–1643?)

PIKE

Pike, three inches long, perfect
Pike in all parts, green tigering the gold.
Killers from the egg: the malevolent aged grin.
They dance on the surface among the flies.

Or move, stunned by their own grandeur,
Over a bed of emerald, silhouette
Of submarine delicacy and horror.
A hundred feet long in their world.

In ponds, under the heat-struck lily pads –
Gloom of their stillness:
Logged on last year's black leaves, watching upwards.
Or hung in an amber cavern of weeds.

The jaws' hooked clamp and fangs
Not to be changed at this date;
A life subdued to its instrument;
The gills kneading quietly, and the pectorals.

Three we kept behind glass,
Jungled in weed: three inches, four,
And four and a half: fed fry to them –
Suddenly there were two. Finally one

With a sag belly and the grin it was born with.
And indeed they spare nobody.
Two, six pounds each, over two feet long,
High and dry and dead in the willow-herb –

One jammed past its gills down the other's gullet:
The outside eye stared: as a vice locks –
The same iron in this eye
Though its film shrank in death.

A pond I fished, fifty yards across,
Whose lilies and muscular tench
Had outlasted every visible stone
Of the monastery that planted them –

Stilled legendary depth:
It was as deep as England. It held
Pike too immense to stir, so immense and old
That past nightfall I dared not cast

But silently cast and fished
With the hair frozen on my head
For what might move, for what eye might move.
The still splashes on the dark pond,

Owls hushing the floating woods
Frail on my ear against the dream
Darkness beneath night's darkness had freed,
That rose slowly towards me, watching.

Ted Hughes (1930–)

WODWO

What am I? Nosing here, turning leaves over
Following a faint stain on the air to the river's edge
I enter water. What am I to split
The glassy grain of water looking upward I see the bed
Of the river above me upside down very clear
What am I doing here in mid-air? Why do I find
this frog so interesting as I inspect its most secret
interior and make it my own? Do these weeds
know me and name me to each other have they
seen me before, do I fit in their world? I seem
separate from the ground and not rooted but dropped
out of nothing casually I've no threads
fastening me to anything I can go anywhere
I seem to have been given the freedom
of this place what am I then? And picking
bits of bark off this rotten stump gives me
no pleasure and it's no use so why do I do it
me and doing that have coincided very queerly
But what shall I be called am I the first
have I an owner what shape am I what
shape am I am I huge if I go
to the end on this way past these trees and past these trees
till I get tired that's touching one wall of me
for the moment if I sit still how everything
stops to watch me I suppose I am the exact centre
but there's all this what is it roots
roots roots roots and here's the water
again very queer but I'll go on looking

Ted Hughes (1930–)

Wodwo trolls of the forest. In Old English *wod* (wood) means 'mad'.

from **THE WHITE DEVIL, V, iv**

FIELD FUNERAL

Call for the robin-redbreast and the wren,
    Since o'er shady groves they hover,
    And with leaves and flowers do cover
The friendless bodies of unburied men.
    Call unto his funeral dole
    The ant, the field-mouse, and the mole,
To rear him hillocks that shall keep him warm
And (when gay tombs are robbed) sustain no harm;
But keep the wolf far thence, that's foe to men,
For with his nails he'll dig them up again.

John Webster (1580?–1625?)

GREEN THOUGHTS

Annihilating all that's made
To a green thought in a green shade

Andrew Marvell, 'The Garden'

The poet holds the mirror up to nature, says Hamlet in his speech to the players. What he or she captures is not a photograph but an image of reality mediated by all the faculties of the beholder. 'Felt in the blood, and felt along the heart' says Wordsworth; 'No axioms but those which have been felt on the pulses' says Keats; 'Mixing memory and desire . . . What are the roots that clutch?' says Eliot.

This section includes some famous symphonic meditations on nature, from Marvell's 'Garden', Gray's 'Elegy' and Wordsworth's 'Tintern Abbey' to more recent examples of the genre. (Matthew Arnold's 'Dover Beach', Keats's 'Ode to Autumn' and other poems scattered throughout this book might also have found a place here.) In them the poets brood on the splendours and uncertainties of our relationship to the earth.

THE GARDEN

How vainly men themselves amaze
To win the palm, the oak, or bays,
And their uncessant labours see
Crowned from some single herb or tree,
Whose short and narrow vergèd shade
Does prudently their toils upbraid,
While all flow'rs and all trees do close
To weave the garlands of repose.

Fair Quiet, have I found thee here,
And Innocence, thy sister dear!
Mistaken long, I sought you then
In busy companies of men.
Your sacred plants, if here below,
Only among the plants will grow.
Society is all but rude,
To this delicious solitude.

No white nor red was ever seen
So am'rous as this lovely green.
Fond lovers, cruel as their flame,
Cut in these trees their mistress' name.
Little, alas, they know, or heed,
How far these beauties hers exceed!
Fair trees! wheres'e'er your barks I wound,
No name shall but your own be found.

When we have run our passion's heat,
Love hither makes his best retreat.
The gods, that mortal beauty chase,
Still in a tree did end their race.
Apollo hunted Daphne so,
Only that she might laurel grow.
And Pan did after Syrinx speed,
Not as a nymph, but for a reed.

What wondrous life is this I lead!
Ripe apples drop about my head;
The luscious clusters of the vine
Upon my mouth do crush their wine;
The nectarene, and curious peach,
Into my hands themselves do reach;
Stumbling on melons, as I pass,
Ensnared with flowers, I fall on grass.

Meanwhile the mind, from pleasure less,
Withdraws into its happiness:
The mind, that ocean where each kind
Does straight its own resemblance find,
Yet it creates, transcending these,
Far other worlds, and other seas,
Annihilating all that's made
To a green thought in a green shade.

Here at the fountain's sliding foot,
Or at some fruit-tree's mossy root,
Casting the body's vest aside,
My soul into the boughs does glide:
There like a bird it sits, and sings,
Then whets, and combs its silver wings;
And, till prepared for longer flight,
Waves in its plumes the various light.

Such was that happy garden-state,
While man there walked without a mate:
After a place so pure, and sweet,
What other help could yet be meet!
But 'twas beyond a mortal's share
To wander solitary there:
Two paradises 'twere in one
To live in paradise alone.

How well the skilful gardener drew
Of flowers and herbs this dial new,
Where from above the milder sun
Does through a fragrant zodiac run;
And, as it works, the industrious bee
Computes its time as well as we.
How could such sweet and wholesome hours
Be reckoned but with herbs and flowers!

Andrew Marvell (1621–1678)

JERUSALEM

And did those feet in ancient time
Walk upon England's mountains green?
And was the holy Lamb of God
On England's pleasant pastures seen?

And did the Countenance Divine
Shine forth upon our clouded hills?
And was Jerusalem builded here
Among these dark Satanic Mills?

Bring me my Bow of burning gold:
Bring me my Arrows of desire:
Bring me my Spear: O clouds unfold!
Bring me my Chariot of fire.

I will not cease from Mental Fight,
Nor shall my Sword sleep in my hand
Till we have built Jerusalem
In England's green and pleasant Land.

William Blake (1757–1827)

from **ELEGY**

The Curfew tolls the knell of parting day,
The lowing herd wind slowly oe'r the lea,
The ploughman homeward plods his weary way,
And leaves the world to darkness and to me.

Now fades the glimmering landscape on the sight,
And all the air a solemn stillness holds,
Save where the beetle wheels his droning flight,
And drowsy tinklings lull the distant folds;

Save that from yonder ivy-mantled tow'r
The moping owl does to the moon complain
Of such, as wand'ring near her secret bow'r,
Molest her ancient solitary reign.

Beneath those rugged elms, that yew-tree's shade,
Where heaves the turf in many a mould'ring heap,
Each in his narrow cell for ever laid,
The rude Forefathers of the hamlet sleep.

The breezy call of incense-breathing Morn,
The swallow twitt'ring from the straw-built shed,
The cock's shrill clarion, or the echoing horn,
No more shall rouse them from their lowly bed.

For them no more the blazing hearth shall burn,
Or busy housewife ply her evening care:
No children run to lisp their sire's return,
Or climb his knees the envied kiss to share.

Oft did the harvest to their sickle yield,
Their furrow oft the stubborn glebe has broke;
How jocund did they drive their team afield!
How bow'd the woods beneath their sturdy stroke!

Let not Ambition mock their useful toil,
Their homely joys, and destiny obscure;
Nor Grandeur hear with a disdainful smile,
The short and simple annals of the poor.

The boast of heraldry, the pomp of pow'r,
And all that beauty, all that wealth e'er gave,
Awaits alike th' inevitable hour.
The paths of glory lead but to the grave.

*   *   *

Far from the madding crowd's ignoble strife,
Their sober wishes never learn'd to stray;
Along the cool sequester'd vale of life
They kept the noiseless tenor of their way.

Yet ev'n these bones from insult to protect
Some frail memorial still erected nigh,
With uncouth rhymes and shapeless sculpture deck'd,
Implores the passing tribute of a sigh.

Their name, their years, spelt by th' unletter'd muse,
The place of fame and elegy supply:
And many a holy text around she strews,
That teach the rustic moralist to die.

For who to dumb Forgetfulness a prey,
This pleasing anxious being e'er resign'd,
Left the warm precincts of the cheerful day,
Nor cast one longing ling'ring look behind?

On some fond breast the parting soul relies,
Some pious drops the closing eye requires;
Ev'n from the tomb the voice of Nature cries,
Ev'n in our Ashes live their wonted Fires.

For thee, who mindful of th' unhonour'd Dead
Dost in these lines their artless tale relate;
If chance, by lonely contemplation led,
Some kindred Spirit shall inquire thy fate,

Haply some hoary-headed Swain may say,
'Oft have we seen him at the peep of dawn
Brushing with hasty steps the dews away
To meet the sun upon the upland lawn.

'There at the foot of yonder nodding beech
That wreathes its old fantastic roots so high,
His listless length at noontide would he stretch,
And pore upon the brook that babbles by.

'Hard by yon wood, now smiling as in scorn,
Mutt'ring his wayward fancies he would rove,
Now drooping, woeful wan, like one forlorn,
Or craz'd with care, or cross'd in hopeless love.

'One morn I miss'd him on the custom'd hill,
Along the heath and near his fav'rite tree;
Another came; nor yet beside the rill,
Nor up the lawn, nor at the wood was he;

'The next with dirges due in sad array
Slow thro' the church-way path we saw him borne.
Approach and read (for thou can'st read) the lay,
Grav'd on the stone beneath yon aged thorn.'

(There scatter'd oft, the earliest of the year,
By Hands unseen, are show'rs of Violets found;
The Red-breast loves to build and warble there,
And little Footsteps lightly print the Ground.)

THE EPITAPH

Here rests his head upon the lap of Earth
A Youth to Fortune and to Fame unknown.
Fair Science frown'd not on his humble birth,
And Melancholy mark'd him for her own.

Large was his bounty, and his soul sincere,
Heav'n did a recompense as largely send:
He gave to Mis'ry all he had, a tear,
He gain'd from Heav'n ('twas all he wish'd) a friend.

No farther seek his merits to disclose,
Or draw his frailties from their dread abode,
(There they alike in trembling hope repose,)
The bosom of his Father and his God.

Thomas Gray (1716–1771)

GOD'S OMNIPOTENCE

Ancient of Days! to Whom all times are Now;
   Before Whom Seraphim do bow,
Though highest creatures, yet to their Creator low.

Who art by light-surrounded powers obeyed
   (Heav'n's host Thy minist'ring spirits made),
Clothed with ubiquity, to Whom all light is shade!

Whose thunder-clasping Hand does grasp the shoal
   Of total Nature, and unroll
The spangled canopy of Heav'n from pole to pole!

Who, on the clouds and winds, Thy chariot, rid'st:
   And, bridling wildest storms, them guid'st;
Who, moveless, all does move, who, changing all, abid'st!

Edward Benlowes (1603–1676)

DAYS

What are days for?
Days are where we live.
They come, they wake us
Time and time over.
They are to be happy in:
Where can we live but days?

Ah, solving that question
Brings the priest and the doctor
In their long coats
Running over the fields.

Philip Larkin (1922–1985)

TINTERN ABBEY

from LINES

*Written a few miles above Tintern Abbey,
on revisiting the banks of the Wye during a tour.
July 13, 1798*

Five years have passed; five summers, with the length
Of five long winters! and again I hear
These waters, rolling from their mountain-springs
With a sweet inland murmur – Once again
Do I behold these steep and lofty cliffs,
Which on a wild secluded scene impress
Thoughts of more deep seclusion; and connect
The landscape with the quiet of the sky.
The day is come when I again repose
Here, under this dark sycamore, and view
These plots of cottage-ground, these orchard-tufts,
Which, at this season, with their unripe fruits,
Among the woods and copses lose themselves,
Nor, with their green and simple hue, disturb
The wild green landscape. Once again I see
These hedge-rows, hardly hedge-rows, little lines
Of sportive wood run wild; these pastoral farms
Green to the very door; and wreathes of smoke
Sent up, in silence, from among the trees,
With some uncertain notice, as might seem,
Of vagrant dwellers in the houseless woods,
Or of some hermit's cave, where by his fire
The hermit sits alone.
              Though absent long,
These forms of beauty have not been to me,
As is a landscape to a blind man's eye:
But oft, in lonely rooms, and mid the din
Of towns and cities, I have owed to them,

In hours of weariness, sensations sweet,
Felt in the blood, and felt along the heart,
And passing even into my purer mind,
With tranquil restoration: – feelings too
Of unremembered pleasure: such, perhaps,
As may have had no trivial influence
On that best portion of a good man's life,
His little, nameless, unremembered acts
Of kindness and of love. Nor less, I trust,
To them I may have owed another gift,
Of aspect more sublime; that blessed mood,
In which the burthen of the mystery,
In which the heavy and the weary weight
Of all this unintelligible world
Is lighten'd – that serene and blessed mood,
In which the affections gently lead us on,
Until, the breath of this corporeal frame,
And even the motion of our human blood
Almost suspended, we are laid asleep
In body, and become a living soul:
While with an eye made quiet by the power
Of harmony, and the deep power of joy,
We see into the life of things.
                                        If this
Be but a vain belief, yet, oh! how oft,
In darkness, and amid the many shapes
Of joyless day-light; when the fretful stir
Unprofitable, and the fever of the world,
Have hung upon the beatings of my heart,
How oft, in spirit, have I turned to thee,
O sylvan Wye! Thou wanderer through the woods,
How often has my spirit turned to thee!

    And now, with gleams of half-extinguish'd thought,
With many recognitions dim and faint,
And somewhat of a sad perplexity,

The picture of the mind revives again:
While here I stand, not only with the sense
Of present pleasure, but with pleasing thoughts
That in this moment there is life and food
For future years. And so I dare to hope,
Though changed, no doubt, from what I was, when first
I came among these hills; when like a roe
I bounded o'er the mountains, by the sides
Of the deep rivers, and the lonely streams,
Wherever nature led: more like a man
Flying from something that he dreads, than one
Who sought the thing he loved. For nature then
(The coarser pleasures of my boyish days,
And their glad animal movements all gone by,)
To me was all in all. – I cannot paint
What then I was. The sounding cataract
Haunted me like a passion: the tall rock,
The mountain, and the deep and gloomy wood,
Their colours and their forms, were then to me
An appetite: a feeling and a love,
That had no need of a remoter charm,
By thought supplied, or any interest
Unborrowed from the eye. – That time is past,
And all its aching joys are now no more,
And all its dizzy raptures. Not for this
Faint I, nor mourn nor murmur: other gifts
Have followed, for such loss, I would believe,
Abundant recompense. For I have learned
To look on nature, not as in the hour
Of thoughtless youth, but hearing oftentimes
The still, sad music of humanity,
Nor harsh nor grating, though of ample power
To chasten and subdue. And I have felt
A presence that disturbs me with the joy
Of elevated thoughts; a sense sublime
Of something far more deeply interfused,

Whose dwelling is the light of setting suns,
And the round ocean, and the living air,
And the blue sky, and in the mind of man,
A motion and a spirit, that impels
All thinking things, all objects of all thoughts,
And rolls through all things. Therefore am I still
A lover of the meadows and the woods,
And mountains; and of all that we behold
From this green earth; of all the mighty world
Of eye and ear, both what they half create,
And what perceive; well pleased to recognise
In nature and the language of the sense,
The anchor of my purest thoughts, the nurse,
The guide, the guardian of my heart, and soul
Of all my moral being.

William Wordsworth (1770–1850)

FROST AT MIDNIGHT

The Frost performs its secret ministry,
Unhelped by any wind. The owlet's cry
Came loud – and hark, again! loud as before.
The inmates of my cottage, all at rest,
Have left me to that solitude, which suits
Abstruser musings: save that at my side
My cradled infant slumbers peacefully.
'Tis calm indeed! so calm, that it disturbs
And vexes meditation with its strange
And extreme silentness. Sea, hill, and wood.
This populous village! Sea, and hill, and wood,
With all the numberless goings-on of life,
Inaudible as dreams! the thin blue flame
Lies on my low-burnt fire, and quivers not;
Only that film, which fluttered on the grate,
Still flutters there, the sole unquiet thing.
Methinks, its motion in this hush of nature
Gives it dim sympathies with me who live,
Making it a companionable form,
Whose puny flaps and freaks the idling Spirit
By its own moods interprets, every where
Echo or mirror seeking of itself,
And makes a toy of Thought.

                But O! how oft,
How oft, at school, with most believing mind,
Presageful, have I gazed upon the bars,
To watch that fluttering *stranger*! and as oft
With unclosed lids, already had I dreamt
Of my sweet birth-place, and the old church-tower,
Whose bells, the poor man's only music, rang
From morn to evening, all the hot Fair-day,
So sweetly, that they stirred and haunted me
With a wild pleasure, falling on mine ear

Most like articulate sounds of things to come!
So gazed I, till the soothing things, I dreamt,
Lulled me to sleep, and sleep prolonged my dreams!
And so I brooded all the following morn,
Awed by the stern preceptor's face, mine eye
Fixed with mock study on my swimming book:
Save if the door half opened, and I snatched
A hasty glance, and still my heart leaped up,
For still I hoped to see the *stranger's* face,
Townsman, or aunt, or sister more beloved,
My play-mate when we both were clothed alike!

Dear Babe, that sleepest cradled by my side,
Whose gentle breathings, heard in this deep calm,
Fill up the interspersed vacancies
And momentary pauses of the thought!
My babe so beautiful! it thrills my heart
With tender gladness, thus to look at thee,
And think that thou shalt learn far other lore,
And in far other scenes! For I was reared
In the great city, pent 'mid cloisters dim,
And saw nought lovely but the sky and stars.
But *thou*, my babe! shalt wander like a breeze
By lakes and sandy shores, beneath the crags
Of ancient mountain, and beneath the clouds,
Which image in their bulk both lakes and shores
And mountain crags: so shalt thou see and hear
The lovely shapes and sounds intelligible
Of that eternal language, which thy God
Utters, who from eternity doth teach
Himself in all, and all things in himself.
Great universal Teacher! he shall mould
Thy spirit, and by giving make it ask.

Therefore all seasons shall be sweet to thee,
Whether the summer clothe the general earth

With greenness, or the redbreast sit and sing
Betwixt the tufts of snow on the bare branch
Of mossy apple-tree, while the nigh thatch
Smokes in the sun-thaw; whether the eave-drops fall
Heard only in the trances of the blast,
Or if the secret ministry of frost
Shall hang them up in silent icicles,
Quietly shining to the quiet Moon.

S. T. Coleridge (1772–1834)

GOD'S GRANDEUR

The world is charged with the grandeur of God.
    It will flame out, like shining from shook foil;
    It gathers to a greatness, like the ooze of oil
Crushed. Why do men then now not reck his rod?
Generations have trod, have trod, have trod;
    And all is seared with trade; bleared, smeared with toil;
    And wears man's smudge and shares man's smell: the soil
Is bare now, nor can foot feel, being shod.

And for all this, nature is never spent;
    There lives the dearest freshness deep down things;
And though the last lights off the black West went
    Oh, morning, at the brown brink eastward, springs –
Because the Holy Ghost over the bent
    World broods with warm breast and with ah! bright wings.

Gerard Manley Hopkins (1844–1889)

from PARADISE LOST

BOOK IV

So on he fares, and to the border comes
Of Eden, where delicious Paradise,
Now nearer, crowns with her enclosure green,
As with a rural mound the champaign head
Of a steep wilderness, whose hairy sides
With thicket overgrown, grotesque and wild,
Access denied; and over head up grew
Insuperable height of loftiest shade,
Cedar, and Pine, and Fir, and branching Palm,
A sylvan scene, and as the ranks ascend
Shade above shade, a woody theatre
Of stateliest view. Yet higher than their tops
The verdurous wall of Paradise up sprung:
Which to our general sire gave prospect large
Into his nether empire neighbouring round.
And higher than that wall a circling row
Of goodliest trees laden with fairest fruit,
Blossoms and fruits at once of golden hue
Appeared with gay enamelled colours mixed:
On which the sun more glad impressed his beams
Than in fair evening cloud, or humid bow,
When God hath showered the earth: so lovely seemed
That landscape: And of pure now purer air
Meets his approach, and to the heart inspires
Vernal delight and joy, able to drive
All sadness but despair: now gentle gales
Fanning their odoriferous wings dispense
Native perfumes, and whisper whence they stole
Those balmy spoils.

John Milton (1608–1674)

A MUSICAL INSTRUMENT

What was he doing, the great god Pan,
Down in the reeds by the river?
Spreading ruin and scattering ban,
Splashing and paddling with hoofs of a goat,
And breaking the golden lilies afloat
With the dragon-fly on the river.

He tore out a reed, the great god Pan,
From the deep cool bed of the river;
The limpid water turbidly ran,
And the broken lilies a-dying lay,
And the dragon-fly had fled away
Ere he brought it out of the river.

High on the shore sat the great god Pan,
While turbidly flowed the river;
And hacked and hewed as a great god can
With his hard bleak steel at the patient reed,
Till there was not a sign of a leaf indeed
To prove it fresh from the river.

He cut it short did the great god Pan
(How tall it stood in the river!)
Then drew the pith, like the heart of a man,
Steadily from the outside ring,
And notched the poor dry empty thing
In holes, as he sat by the river.

'This is the way,' laughed the great god Pan
(Laughed while he sat by the river),
'The only way, since gods began
To make sweet music, they could succeed.'
Then dropping his mouth to a hole in the reed
He blew in power by the river.

Sweet, sweet, sweet, O Pan!
Piercing sweet by the river!
Blinding sweet, O great god Pan!
The sun on the hill forgot to die,
And the lilies revived, and the dragon-fly
Came back to dream on the river.

Yet half a beast is the great god Pan,
To laugh as he sits by the river,
Making a poet out of a man:
The true gods sigh for the cost and pain –
For the reed which grows never more again
As a reed with the reeds of the river.

Elizabeth Barrett Browning (1806–1861)

from AUGURIES OF INNOCENCE

To see a World in a Grain of Sand
And a Heaven in a Wild Flower,
Hold Infinity in the palm of your hand
And Eternity in an hour.

A Robin Redbreast in a Cage
Puts all Heaven in a Rage.
A dove house fill'd with doves and Pigeons
Shudders Hell thro' all its regions.
A dog starv'd at his Master's Gate
Predicts the ruin of the State.
A Horse misus'd upon the Road
Calls to Heaven for Human blood.
Each outcry of the hunted Hare
A fibre from the Brain does tear.

A Skylark wounded in the wing,
A Cherubim does cease to sing.
The Game Cock clip'd and arm'd for fight
Does the Rising Sun affright.
Every Wolf's and Lion's howl
Raises from Hell a Human Soul.
The wild deer, wand'ring here and there,
Keeps the Human Soul from Care.
The Lamb misus'd breeds Public strife
And yet forgives the Butcher's Knife.
The Bat that flits at close of Eve
Has left the Brain that won't Believe.
The Owl that calls upon the Night
Speaks the Unbeliever's fright.
He who shall hurt the little Wren
Shall never be belov'd by Men.
He who the Ox to wrath has mov'd
Shall never be by Woman lov'd.
The wanton Boy that kills the Fly
Shall feel the Spider's enmity.
He who torments the Chafer's sprite
Weaves a Bower in endless Night.

William Blake (1757–1827)

CONSTANCY TO AN IDEAL OBJECT

Since all that beat about in Nature's range,
Or veer or vanish; why should'st thou remain
The only constant in a world of change,
O yearning Thought! that liv'st but in the brain?
Call to the Hours, that in the distance play,
The faery people of the future day –

Fond Thought! not one of all that shining swarm
Will breathe on thee with life-enkindling breath,
Till when, like strangers shelt'ring from a storm,
Hope and Despair meet in the porch of Death!
Yet still thou haunt'st me; and though well I see,
She is not thou, and only thou art she,
Still, still as though some dear embodied Good,
Some living Love before my eyes there stood
With answering look a ready ear to lend,
I mourn to thee and say – 'Ah! loveliest friend!
That this the meed of all my toils might be,
To have a home, an English home, and thee!'
Vain repetition! Home and Thou are one.
The peacefull'st cot, the moon shall shine upon,
Lulled by the thrush and wakened by the lark,
Without thee were but a becalmed bark,
Whose Helmsman on an ocean waste and wide
Sits mute and pale his mouldering helm beside.

And art thou nothing? Such thou art, as when
The woodman winding westward up the glen
At wintry dawn, where o'er the sheep-track's maze
The viewless snow-mist weaves a glist'ning haze,
Sees full before him, gliding without tread,
An image with a glory round its head;
The enamoured rustic worships its fair hues,
Nor knows he makes the shadow, he pursues!

S. T. Coleridge (1772–1834)

ODE ON SOLITUDE

Happy the man, whose wish and care
  A few paternal acres bound,
Content to breathe his native air
        In his own ground.

Whose herds with milk, whose fields with bread,
  Whose flocks supply him with attire;
Whose trees in summer yield him shade,
        In winter fire.

Blest! who can unconcern'dly find
  Hours, days, and years slide soft away
In health of body, peace of mind,
        Quiet by day,

Sound sleep by night; study and ease
  Together mix'd; sweet recreation,
And innocence, which most does please
        With meditation.

Thus let me live, unseen, unknown;
  Thus unlamented let me die;
Steal from the world, and not a stone
        Tell where I lie.

Alexander Pope (1688–1744)

A SHROPSHIRE LAD

XL

Into my heart an air that kills
   From yon far country blows:
What are those blue remembered hills,
   What spires, what farms are those?

That is the land of lost content,
   I see it shining plain,
The happy highways where I went
   And cannot come again.

A. E. Housman (1859–1936)

THE WORLD

The world is too much with us; late and soon,
Getting and spending, we lay waste our powers:
Little we see in nature that is ours;
We have given our hearts away, a sordid boon!
This Sea that bares her bosom to the moon;
The Winds that will be howling at all hours
And are up-gathered now like sleeping flowers;
For this, for every thing, we are out of tune;
It moves us not – Great God! I'd rather be
A Pagan suckled in a creed outworn;
So might I, standing on this pleasant lea,
Have glimpses that would make me less forlorn;
Have sight of Proteus coming from the sea;
Or hear old Triton blow his wreathèd horn.

William Wordsworth (1770–1850)

PIED BEAUTY

Glory be to God for dappled things –
   For skies of couple-colour as a brinded cow;
     For rose-moles all in stipple upon trout that swim;
Fresh firecoal chestnut-falls; finches' wings;
   Landscape plotted and pieced – fold, fallow, and plough;
     And all trades, their gear and tackle and trim.

All things counter, original, spare, strange;
   Whatever is fickle, freckled (who knows how?)
     With swift, slow; sweet, sour; adazzle, dim;
He fathers-forth whose beauty is past change:
               Praise him.

Gerard Manley Hopkins (1844–1889)

EPIGRAM

My soul, what's better than a feather? Wind.
Than wind? The fire. And what than fire? The Mind.
What's higher than the mind? A thought. Than thought?
This bubble world. What than this bubble? Naught.

Francis Quarles (1592–1644)

103

THE RAINBOW

My heart leaps up when I behold
    A Rainbow in the sky:
So was it when my life began;
So is it now I am a Man;
So be it when I shall grow old,
    Or let me die!
The Child is Father of the Man;
And I could wish my days to be
Bound each to each by natural piety.

William Wordsworth (1770–1850)

AUGUST 1914

What in our lives is burnt
In the fire of this?
The heart's dear granary?
The much we shall miss?

Three lives hath one life –
Iron, honey, gold.
The gold, the honey gone –
Left is the hard and cold.

Iron are our lives
Molten right through our youth.
A burnt space through ripe fields
A fair mouth's broken tooth.

Isaac Rosenberg (1890–1918)

OLD SONG

The day is ending, the night descending,
the heart is frozen, the spirit dead;
but the moon is wending her way, attending
to other things that are left unsaid.

D. H. Lawrence (1885–1930)

THE WINDHOVER

To Christ our Lord

I caught this morning morning's minion, king-
    dom of daylight's dauphin, dapple-dawn-drawn Falcon, in his
      riding
  Of the rolling level underneath him steady air, and striding
High there, how he rung upon the rein of a wimpling wing
In his ecstasy! then off, off forth on swing,
    As a skate's heel sweeps smooth on a bow-bend: the hurl and
      gliding
    Rebuffed the big wind. My heart in hiding
Stirred for a bird, – the achieve of, the mastery of the thing!

Brute beauty and valour and act, oh, air, pride, plume, here
  Buckle! AND the fire that breaks from thee then, a billion
Times told lovelier, more dangerous, O my chevalier!

  No wonder of it: sheer plod makes plough down sillion
Shine, and blue-bleak embers, ah my dear,
  Fall, gall themselves, and gash gold-vermilion.

Gerard Manley Hopkins (1844–1889)

from **THE PRELUDE**

BOOK ELEVEN

There are in our existence spots of time,
Which with distinct pre-eminence retain
A vivifying Virtue, whence, depress'd
By false opinion and contentious thought,
Or aught of heavier or more deadly weight,
In trivial occupations, and the round
Of ordinary intercourse, our minds
Are nourished and invisibly repair'd,
A virtue by which pleasure is enhanced,
That penetrates, enables us to mount
When high, more high, and lifts us up when fallen.
This efficacious spirit chiefly lurks
Among those passages of life in which
We have had deepest feeling that the mind
Is lord and master, and that outward sense
Is but the obedient servant of her will.
Such moments, worthy of all gratitude,
Are scatter'd everywhere, taking their date
From our first childhood: in our childhood even
Perhaps are most conspicuous. Life with me,
As far as memory can look back, is full
Of this beneficent influence. At a time
When scarcely (I was then not six years old)
My hand could hold a bridle, with proud hopes
I mounted, and we rode towards the hills:
We were a pair of horsemen; honest James
Was with me, my encourager and guide.
We had not travell'd long, ere some mischance
Disjoin'd me from my Comrade, and, through fear
Dismounting, down the rough and stony Moor
I led my Horse, and stumbling on, at length
Came to a bottom, where in former times

A Murderer had been hung in iron chains.
The Gibbet-mast was moulder'd down, the bones
And iron case were gone; but on the turf,
Hard by, soon after that fell deed was wrought
Some unknown hand had carved the Murderer's name.
The monumental writing was engraven
In times long past, and still, from year to year,
By superstition of the neighbourhood,
The grass is clear'd away; and to this hour
The letters are all fresh and visible.
Faltering, and ignorant where I was, at length
I chanced to espy those characters inscribed
On the green sod: forthwith I left the spot
And, reascending the bare Common, saw
A naked Pool that lay beneath the hills,
The Beacon on the summit, and more near,
A Girl who bore a Pitcher on her head
And seem'd with difficult steps to force her way
Against the blowing wind. It was, in truth,
An ordinary sight; but I should need
Colours and words that are unknown to man
To paint the visionary dreariness
Which, while I look'd all round for my lost guide,
Did at that time invest the naked Pool,
The Beacon on the lonely Eminence,
The Woman, and her garments vex'd and toss'd
By the strong wind.

William Wordsworth (1770–1850)

IN TIME OF 'THE BREAKING OF NATIONS'

Only a man harrowing clods
   In a slow silent walk
With an old horse that stumbles and nods
   Half asleep as they stalk.

Only thin smoke without flame
   From the heaps of couch-grass;
Yet this will go onward the same
   Though Dynasties pass.

Yonder a maid and her wight
   Come whispering by:
War's annals will cloud into night
   Ere their story die.

1915

Thomas Hardy (1840–1928)

from CYMBELINE, IV, ii

FEAR NO MORE

Fear no more the heat o' the sun
    Nor the furious winter's rages;
Thou thy worldly task hast done,
    Home art gone and ta'en thy wages:
Golden lads and girls all must,
As chimney-sweepers, come to dust.

Fear no more the frown o' the great,
    Thou art past the tyrant's stroke;
Care no more to clothe and eat;
    To thee the reed is as the oak:
The sceptre, learning, physic, must
All follow this, and come to dust.

Fear no more the lightning-flash
    Nor the all-dreaded thunder-stone;
Fear not slander, censure rash;
    Thou hast finish'd joy and moan:
All lovers young, all lovers must
Consign to thee, and come to dust.

William Shakespeare (1564–1616)

THE ANGLER'S SONG

Man's life is but vain, for 'tis subject to pain
    And sorrow, and short as a bubble;
'Tis a hodge-podge of business and money and care,
    And care and money and trouble.

But we'll take no care when the weather proves fair,
    Nor will we now vex though it rain;
We'll banish all sorrow, and sing till to-morrow,
    And angle and angle again.

Anon (17th Century?)

LOVE IN A LANDSCAPE

Come live with me and be my Love
And we will all the pleasures prove
That hills and valleys, dales and fields,
Or woods or steepy mountains yields.

Christopher Marlowe, 'The Passionate Shepherd to His Love'

Momentous happenings, epiphanies, Wordsworth's 'spots of time' (a phrase which itself marries space and time) often fuse in our minds with particular locations, and they are charged forever afterwards with an unforgettable intensity. So much so that for a time, or perhaps forever, the normal distinction between inner and outer seems to be obliterated. The 'language of the heart' and 'the picture of the mind' turn out to be creation itself. Whether lovers are star-crossed or strewn with flowers is a matter that seems to involve the entire natural world.

In these poems nature is 'used' in every sense of the word, much as a shaman invokes all the invisible but potent spirits contending for our souls. By aligning our happiness or unhappiness with that of the elements we seek both to explain its origins and to sanction its logic.

Poets were 'green' long before ecologists came along. They were also the earliest and best psychologists, as Freud was happy to acknowledge. They tell it like it is, as the elements do.

Love happens indoors as well as out, for sure, but when we reach for an adequate vocabulary to describe it the most accurate and useful lexicon turns out to be that provided by nature itself.

THE PASSIONATE SHEPHERD
TO HIS LOVE

Come live with me and be my Love,
And we will all the pleasures prove
That hills and valleys, dales and fields,
Or woods or steepy mountains yields.

And we will sit upon the rocks,
And see the shepherds feed their flocks
By shallow rivers, to whose falls
Melodious birds sing madrigals.

And I will make thee beds of roses
And a thousand fragrant posies;
A cap of flowers, and a kirtle
Embroidered all with leaves of myrtle.

A gown made of the finest wool
Which from our pretty lambs we pull;
Fair-lined slippers for the cold,
With buckles of the purest gold.

A belt of straw and ivy-buds
With coral clasps and amber studs:
And if these pleasures may thee move,
Come live with me and be my Love.

The shepherd swains shall dance and sing
For thy delight each May morning:
If these delights thy mind may move,
Then live with me and be my Love.

Christopher Marlowe (1564–1593)

THE NYMPH'S REPLY TO THE SHEPHERD

If all the world and love were young,
And truth in every shepherd's tongue,
These pretty pleasures might me move
To live with thee and be thy Love.

But Time drives flocks from field to fold,
When rivers rage and rocks grow cold,
And Philomel becometh dumb;
The rest complains of cares to come.

The flowers do fade, and wanton fields
To wayward Winter reckoning yields:
A honey tongue, a heart of gall,
Is fancy's spring, but sorrow's fall.

Thy gowns, thy shoes, thy beds of roses,
Thy cap, thy kirtle, and thy posies,
Soon break, soon wither – soon forgotten,
In folly ripe, in reason rotten.

Thy belt of straw and ivy-buds,
Thy coral clasps and amber studs, –
All these in me no means can move
To come to thee and be thy Love.

But could youth last, and love still breed,
Had joys no date, nor age no need,
Then these delights my mind might move
To live with thee and be thy Love.

Sir Walter Ralegh (1552?–1618)

THE SONG OF WANDERING AENGUS

I went out to the hazel wood,
Because a fire was in my head,
And cut and peeled a hazel wand,
And hooked a berry to a thread;
And when white moths were on the wing,
And moth-like stars were flickering out,
I dropped the berry in a stream
And caught a little silver trout.

When I had laid it on the floor
I went to blow the fire aflame,
But something rustled on the floor,
And someone called me by my name:
It had become a glimmering girl
With apple blossom in her hair
Who called me by my name and ran
And faded through the brightening air.

Though I am old with wandering
Through hollow lands and hilly lands,
I will find out where she has gone,
And kiss her lips and take her hands;
And walk among long dappled grass,
And pluck till time and times are done
The silver apples of the moon,
The golden apples of the sun.

W. B. Yeats (1865–1939)

from PASTORALS: SUMMER

See what delights in sylvan scenes appear!
Descending Gods have found *Elysium* here.
In woods bright *Venus* with *Adonis* stray'd,
And chaste *Diana* haunts the forest shade.
Come lovely nymph, and bless the silent hours,
When swains from shearing seek their nightly bow'rs;
When weary reapers quit the sultry field,
And crown'd with corn, their thanks to *Ceres* yield.
This harmless grove no lurking viper hides,
But in my breast the serpent Love abides.
Here bees from blossoms sip the rosy dew,
But your *Alexis* knows no sweets but you.
Oh deign to visit our forsaken seats,
The mossy fountains, and the green retreats!
Where-e'er you walk, cool gales shall fan the glade,
Trees, where you sit, shall crowd into a shade,
Where-e'er you tread, the blushing flow'rs shall rise,
And all things flourish where you turn your eyes.
Oh! how I long with you to pass my days,
Invoke the muses, and resound your praise;
Your praise the birds shall chant in ev'ry grove,
And winds shall waft it to the pow'rs above.
But wou'd you sing, and rival *Orpheus'* strain,
The wond'ring forests soon shou'd dance again,
The moving mountains hear the pow'rful call,
And headlong streams hang list'ning in their fall!
But see, the shepherds shun the noon-day heat,
The lowing herds to murm'ring brooks retreat,
To closer shades the panting flocks remove,
Ye Gods! and is there no relief for Love?
But soon the sun with milder rays descends
To the cool ocean, where his journey ends;

On me Love's fiercer flames for ever prey,
By night he scorches, as he burns by day.

Alexander Pope (1688–1744)

ANOTHER SEPTEMBER

Dreams fled away, this country bedroom, raw
With the touch of the dawn, wrapped in a minor peace,
Hears through an open window the garden draw
Long pitch black breaths, lay bare its apple trees,
Ripe pear trees, brambles, windfall-sweetened soil,
Exhale rough sweetness against the starry slates.
Nearer the river sleeps St John's, all toil
Locked fast inside a dream with iron gates.

Domestic Autumn, like an animal
Long used to handling by those countrymen,
Rubs her kind hide against the bedroom wall
Sensing a fragrant child come back again
– Not this half tolerated consciousness,
Its own cold season never done,
But that unspeaking daughter, growing less
Familiar where we fall asleep as one.

Wakeful moth-wings blunder near a chair,
Toss their light shell at the glass, and go
To inhabit the living starlight. Stranded hair
Stirs on the still linen. It is as though
The black breathing that billows her sleep, her name,
Drugged under judgment, waned and – bearing daggers
And balances – down the lampless darkness they came,
Moving like women: Justice, Truth, such figures.

Thomas Kinsella (1928–)

SONNET

Comming to kisse her lyps, (such grace I found)
    Me seemed I smelt a gardin of sweet flowres:
    that dainty odours from them threw around
    for damzels fit to decke their lovers bowres.
Her lips did smell lyke unto Gillyflowers,
    her ruddy cheekes lyke unto Roses red:
    her snowy browes lyke budded Bellamoures,
    her lovely eyes lyke Pincks but newly spred.
Her goodly bosome lyke a Strawberry bed,
    her neck lyke to a bounch of Cullambynes:
    her breast lyke lillyes, ere theyr leaves be shed,
    her nipples lyke yong blossomed Iessemynes.
Such fragrant flowres doe give most odorous smell,
    but her sweet odour did them all excell.

Edmund Spenser (1552?–1599)

SONNET XVIII

Shall I compare thee to a summer's day?
Thou art more lovely and more temperate:
Rough winds do shake the darling buds of May,
And summer's lease hath all too short a date:
Sometime too hot the eye of heaven shines,
And often is his gold complexion dimmed;
And every fair from fair sometime declines,
By chance, or nature's changing course untrimmed:
But thy eternal summer shall not fade,
Nor lose possession of that fair thou ow'st,
Nor shall death brag thou wander'st in his shade,
When in eternal lines to time thou grow'st;
    So long as men can breathe, or eyes can see,
    So long lives this, and this gives life to thee.

William Shakespeare (1564–1616)

TO THE VIRGINS,
TO MAKE MUCH OF TIME

Gather ye rose-buds while ye may,
    Old Time is still a-flying,
And this same flower that smiles to-day,
    To-morrow will be dying.

The glorious lamp of heaven, the sun,
    The higher he's a-getting
The sooner will his race be run,
    And nearer he's to setting.

That age is best which is the first,
    When youth and blood are warmer;
But being spent, the worse, and worst
    Times still succeed the former.

Then be not coy, but use your time;
    And while ye may, go marry:
For having lost but once your prime,
    You may for ever tarry.

Robert Herrick (1591–1674)

from A CELEBRATION OF CHARIS
IN TEN LYRIC PIECES

HER TRIUMPH

Have you seen but a bright lily grow,
  Before rude hands have touched it?
Ha' you marked but the fall o' the snow
  Before the soil hath smutched it?
Ha' you felt the wool o' the beaver,
  Or swansdown ever?
Or have smelt o' the bud o' the briar,
  Or the nard in the fire?
Or have tasted the bag of the bee?
O so white! O so soft! O so sweet is she!

Ben Jonson (1572–1637)

SONNET

With how sad steps, O moon, thou climb'st the skies!
How silently, and with how wan a face!
What! may it be, that even in heav'nly place
That busy archer his sharp arrows tries?
Sure, if that long-with-love-acquainted eyes
Can judge of love, thou feel'st a lover's case;
I read it in thy looks; thy languished grace
To me, that feel the like, thy state descries.
Then, even of fellowship, O moon, tell me,
Is constant love deemed there but want of wit?
Are beauties there as proud as here they be?
Do they above love to be loved, and yet
    Those lovers scorn whom that love doth possess?
    Do they call virtue there ungratefulness?

Sir Philip Sidney (1554–1586)

TWICKNAM GARDEN

Blasted with sighs, and surrounded with tears,
    Hither I come to seek the spring,
    And at mine eyes, and at mine ears,
Receive such balms, as else cure everything;
    But O, self traitor, I do bring
The spider love, which transubstantiates all,
    And can convert manna to gall,
And that this place may thoroughly be thought
    True paradise, I have the serpent brought.

'Twere wholesomer for me, that winter did
    Benight the glory of this place,
    And that a grave frost did forbid
These trees to laugh, and mock me to my face;
    But that I may not this disgrace
Endure, nor yet leave loving, Love, let me
    Some senseless piece of this place be;
Make me a mandrake, so I may groan here,
    Or a stone fountain weeping out my year.

Hither with crystal vials, lovers come,
    And take my tears, which are love's wine,
And try your mistress' tears at home,
For all are false, that taste not just like mine;
    Alas, hearts do not in eyes shine,
Nor can you more judge woman's thoughts by tears,
    Than by her shadow, what she wears.
O perverse sex, where none is true but she,
    Who's therefore true, because her truth kills me.

John Donne (1572–1631)

LINES

I

The cold earth slept below,
   Above the cold sky shone;
And all around, with a chilling sound,
   From caves of ice and fields of snow,
   The breath of night like death did flow
    Beneath the sinking moon.

II

The wintry hedge was black,
   The green grass was not seen,
The birds did rest on the bare thorn's breast,
   Whose roots, beside the pathway track,
   Had bound their folds o'er many a crack,
    Which the frost had made between.

III

Thine eyes glowed in the glare
   Of the moon's dying light;
As a fenfire's beam on a sluggish stream
   Gleams dimly, so the moon shone there,
   And it yellowed the strings of thy raven hair,
    That shook in the wind of night.

IV

The moon made thy lips pale, beloved –
   The wind made thy bosom chill –
The night did shed on thy dear head
   Its frozen dew, and thou didst lie
   Where the bitter breath of the naked sky
    Might visit thee at will.

Percy Bysshe Shelley (1792–1822)

NEUTRAL TONES

We stood by a pond that winter day,
And the sun was white, as though chidden of God,
And a few leaves lay on the starving sod;
     – They had fallen from an ash, and were gray.

Your eyes on me were as eyes that rove
Over tedious riddles of years ago;
And some words played between us to and fro
     On which lost the more by our love.

The smile on your mouth was the deadest thing
Alive enough to have strength to die;
And a grin of bitterness swept thereby
     Like an ominous bird a-wing . . .

Since then, keen lessons that love deceives,
And wrings with wrong, have shaped to me
Your face, and the God-curst sun, and a tree,
     And a pond edged with grayish leaves.

Thomas Hardy (1840–1928)

WALY, WALY

O waly, waly, up the bank,
    And waly, waly, doun the brae;
And waly, waly, yon burn-side,
    Where I and my Love wont to gae!
I leaned my back unto an aik,
    I thocht it was a trustie tree;
But first it bowed and syne it brak –
    Sae my true love did lichtlie me.

O waly, waly, gin love be bonnie
    A little time while it is new!
But when 'tis auld it waxeth cauld,
    And fades awa' like morning dew.
O wherefore should I busk my heid,
    O wherefore should I kame my hair?
For my true Love has me forsook,
    And says he'll never lo'e me mair.

Now Arthur's Seat sall be my bed,
    The sheets sall ne'er be 'filed by me;
Saint Anton's well sall be my drink;
    Since my true Love has forsaken me.
Marti'mas wind, when wilt thou blaw,
    And shake the green leaves aff the tree?
O gentle Death, when wilt thou come?
    For of my life I am wearie.

'Tis not the frost that freezes fell,
    Nor blawing snaw's inclemency;
'Tis not sic cauld that makes me cry,
    But my Love's heart grown cauld to me.
When we came in by Glasgow Town,
    We were a comely sight to see;
My Love was cled in the black velvet,
    And I mysel in cramasie.

But had I wist before I kis'd,
　That Love had been sae ill to win,
I'd lock'd my heart in a case of gold,
　And pin'd it with a siller pin.
Oh oh! if my young babe were born,
　And set upon the nurse's knee,
And I mysel were dead and gane,
　For a maid again I'll never be.

Anon (16th Century?)

cramasie crimson

SONG

When I am dead, my dearest,
　Sing no sad songs for me;
Plant thou no roses at my head;
　Nor shady cypress tree:
Be the green grass above me
　With showers and dewdrops wet;
And if thou wilt, remember,
　And if thou wilt, forget.

I shall not see the shadows,
　I shall not feel the rain;
I shall not hear the nightingale
　Sing on, as if in pain;
And dreaming through the twilight
　That doth not rise nor set,
Haply I may remember,
　And haply may forget.

Christina Rossetti (1830–1894)

SONG

Go, lovely Rose!
Tell her, that wastes her time and me,
   That now she knows,
When I resemble her to thee,
How sweet and fair she seems to be.

Tell her that's young
And shuns to have her graces spied,
   That hadst thou sprung
In deserts, where no men abide,
Thou must have uncommended died.

Small is the worth
Of beauty from the light retired:
   Bid her come forth,
Suffer herself to be desired,
And not blush so to be admired.

Then die! that she
The common fate of all things rare
   May read in thee:
How small a part of time they share
That are so wondrous sweet and fair!

Edmund Waller (1606–1687)

SONG

O my Luve's like a red, red rose
   That's newly sprung in June:
O my Luve's like the melodie
   That's sweetly play'd in tune.

As fair art thou, my bonnie lass,
   So deep in luve am I:
And I will luve thee still, my dear,
   Till a' the seas gang dry:

Till a' the seas gang dry, my dear,
   And the rocks melt wi' the sun;
I will luve thee still, my dear,
   While the sands o' life shall run.

And fare thee weel, my only Luve!
   And fare thee weel a while!
And I will come again, my Luve,
   Tho' it were ten thousand mile.

Robert Burns (1759–1796)

LA BELLE DAME SANS MERCI. A BALLAD

O what can ail thee, knight-at-arms,
    Alone and palely loitering?
The sedge has withered from the lake,
    And no birds sing.

O what can ail thee, knight-at-arms,
    So haggard and so woe-begone?
The squirrel's granary is full,
    And the harvest's done.

I see a lily on thy brow,
    With anguish moist a fever-dew,
And on thy cheeks a fading rose
    Fast withereth too.

I met a lady in the meads,
    Full beautiful – a faery's child,
Her hair was long, her foot was light,
    And her eyes were wild.

I made a garland for her head,
    And bracelets too, and fragrant zone;
She looked at me as she did love,
    And made sweet moan.

I set her on my pacing steed,
    And nothing else saw all day long,
For sidelong would she bend, and sing
    A faery's song.

She found me roots of relish sweet,
    And honey wild, and manna-dew,
And sure in language strange she said –
    'I love thee true'.

She took me to her elfin grot,
　　And there she wept and sighed full sore,
And there I shut her wild wild eyes
　　With kisses four.

And there she lullèd me asleep
　　And there I dreamed – Ah! woe betide! –
The latest dream I ever dreamt
　　On the cold hill side.

I saw pale kings and princes too,
　　Pale warriors, death-pale were they all;
They cried – 'La Belle Dame sans Merci
　　Hath thee in thrall!'

I saw their starved lips in the gloam,
　　With horrid warning gapèd wide,
And I awoke and found me here,
　　On the cold hill's side.

And this is why I sojourn here
　　Alone and palely loitering,
Though the sedge is withered from the lake,
　　And no birds sing.

John Keats (1795–1821)

THE MOWER TO THE GLOW-WORMS

Ye living lamps, by whose dear light
The nightingale does sit so late,
And studying all the summer night,
Her matchless songs does meditate;

Ye country comets, that portend
No war, nor prince's funeral,
Shining unto no higher end
Than to presage the grass's fall;

Ye glow-worms, whose officious flame
To wandering mowers shows the way,
That in the night have lost their aim,
And after foolish fires do stray;

Your courteous lights in vain you waste,
Since *Juliana* here is come,
For she my mind hath so displaced
That I shall never find my home.

Andrew Marvell (1621–1678)

[LUCY]

I

Strange fits of passion I have known,
And I will dare to tell,
But in the lover's ear alone,
What once to me befell.

When she I lov'd was strong and gay
And like a rose in June,
I to her cottage bent my way,
Beneath the evening moon.

Upon the moon I fix'd my eye,
All over the wide lea;
My horse trudg'd on, and we drew nigh
Those paths so dear to me.

And now we reach'd the orchard plot,
And, as we climb'd the hill,
Towards the roof of Lucy's cot
The moon descended still.

In one of those sweet dreams I slept,
Kind Nature's gentlest boon!
And, all the while, my eyes I kept
On the descending moon.

My horse mov'd on; hoof after hoof
He rais'd and never stopp'd:
When down behind the cottage roof
At once the planet dropp'd.

What fond and wayward thoughts will slide
Into a Lover's head –
'O mercy!' to myself I cried,
'If Lucy should be dead!'

II

She dwelt among th' untrodden ways
   Beside the springs of Dove,
A Maid whom there were none to praise
   And very few to love.

A Violet by a mossy stone
   Half-hidden from the Eye!
– Fair, as a star when only one
   Is shining in the sky!

She *liv'd* unknown, and few could know
   When Lucy ceas'd to be;
But she is in her Grave, and Oh!
   The difference to me.

III

A slumber did my spirit seal,
   I had no human fears:
She seem'd a thing that could not feel
   The touch of earthly years.

No motion has she now, no force;
   She neither hears nor sees,
Roll'd round in earth's diurnal course
   With rocks and stones and trees!

William Wordsworth (1770–1850)

from THE PRINCESS

Now sleeps the crimson petal, now the white
Nor waves the cypress in the palace walk;
Nor winks the gold fin in the porphyry font:
The fire-fly wakens: waken thou with me.

Now droops the milkwhite peacock like a ghost,
And like a ghost she glimmers on to me.

Now lies the Earth all Danaë to the stars,
And all thy heart lies open unto me.

Now slides the silent meteor on, and leaves
A shining furrow, as thy thoughts in me.

Now folds the lily all her sweetness up,
And slips into the bosom of the lake:
So fold thyself, my dearest, thou, and slip
Into my bosom and be lost in me.

Alfred Lord Tennyson (1809–1892)

THE RATTLE BAG

As I lay, fullness of praise,
On a summer day under
Trees between field and mountain
Awaiting my soft-voiced girl,
She came, there's no denying,
Where she vowed, a very moon.
Together we sat, fine theme,
The girl and I, debating,
Trading, while I had the right,
Words with the splendid maiden.

And so we were, she was shy,
Learning to love each other,
Concealing sin, winning mead,
An hour lying together,
And then, cold comfort, it came,
A blare, a bloody nuisance,
A sack's bottom's foul seething
From an imp in shepherd's shape,
Who had, public enemy,
A harsh-horned sag-cheeked rattle.
He played, cramped yellow belly,
This bag, curse its scabby leg.
So before satisfaction
The sweet girl panicked: poor me!
When she heard, feeble-hearted,
The stones whir, she would not stay.

By Christ, no Christian country,
Cold harsh tune, has heard the like.
Noisy pouch perched on a pole,
Bell of pebbles and gravel,
Saxon rocks making music
Quaking in a bullock's skin,

Crib of three thousand beetles,
Commotion's cauldron, black bag,
Field-keeper, comrade of straw,
Black-skinned, pregnant with splinters,
Noise that's an old buck's loathing,
Devil's bell, stake in its crotch,
Scarred pebble-bearing belly,
May it be sliced into thongs.
May the churl be struck frigid,
Amen, who scared off my girl.

Dafydd ap Gwillym (flourished 1340–1370)
Translated from the Welsh by Joseph Clancy

from HAMLET, IV, vii

DEATH OF OPHELIA

There is a willow grows aslant a brook
That shows his hoar leaves in the glassy stream;
There with fantastic garlands did she come,
Of crow-flowers, nettles, daisies, and long purples,
That liberal shepherds give a grosser name,
But our cold maids do dead men's fingers call them:
There, on the pendent boughs her coronet weeds
Clambering to hang, an envious sliver broke,
When down her weedy trophies and herself
Fell in the weeping brook. Her clothes spread wide,
And, mermaid-like, awhile they bore her up;
Which time she chanted snatches of old tunes,
As one incapable of her own distress,
Or like a creature native and indu'd
Unto that element; but long it could not be
Till that her garments, heavy with their drink,
Pull'd the poor wretch from her melodious lay
To muddy death.

William Shakespeare (1564–1616)

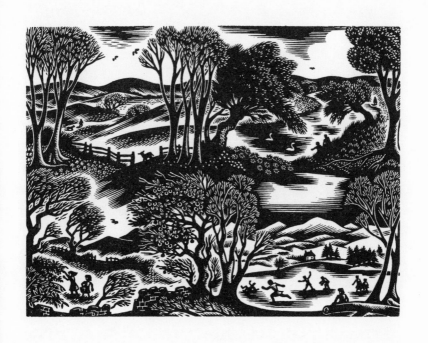

ELEMENTS AND SEASONS

Therefore all seasons shall be sweet to thee...

S. T. Coleridge, 'Frost at Midnight'

There are four of each, or so we say, though I have allowed myself to add a few complementary ones, such as silence and time. Both nouns have their indispensable adjectives, 'elemental' and 'seasonal', which effortlessly translate into descriptions and allegories of our own spiritual, emotional and physical lives. 'Energy is eternal delight' says Blake; hence our endless fascination with rivers and waterfalls, sun, wind, thunder, lightning and stubborn earth. It follows from Blake's aphorism that energy has its own morality, which precedes man-made rules of right and wrong, justice and injustice.

Artistic creation might also be held to conform to Blake's axiom: the greatest works are precisely those which have the most energy sizzling through them.

As for the seasons, English poetry almost lives by them, from 'Sumer is icumen in' and 'When icicles hang by the wall' to any contemporary lyric or pop song you care to name. Like space and time, the seasons are not just labels but aspects of experience itself – heartbeats of consciousness since consciousness began.

WESTRON WYND

Westron wynd, when wyll thow blow,
The small rayne downe can rayne?
Cryst, yf my love were in my armys,
And I yn my bed agayne!

Anon (16th Century)

SONNET LXV

Since brass, nor stone, nor earth, nor boundless sea,
But sad mortality o'ersways their power,
How with this rage shall beauty hold a plea,
Whose action is no stronger than a flower?
O! how shall summer's honey breath hold out
Against the wrackful siege of battering days,
When rocks impregnable are not so stout,
Nor gates of steel so strong, but Time decays?
O fearful meditation! where, alack,
Shall Time's best jewel from Time's chest lie hid?
Or what strong hand can hold his swift foot back?
Or who his spoil of beauty can forbid?
    O, none, unless this miracle have might,
      That in black ink my love may still shine bright.

William Shakespeare (1564–1616)

TIME EATING

Ravenous Time has flowers for his food
in Autumn, yet can cleverly make good
each petal: devours animals and men,
but for ten dead he can create ten.

If you enquire how secretly you've come
to mansize from the smallness of a stone
it will appear his effort made you rise
so gradually to your proper size.

But as he makes he eats; the very part
where he began, even the elusive heart,
Time's ruminative tongue will wash
and slow juice masticate all flesh.

That volatile huge intestine holds
material and abstract in its folds:
thought and ambition melt and even the world
will alter, in that catholic belly curled.

But Time, who ate my love, you cannot make
such another; you who can remake
the lizard's tail and the bright snakeskin
cannot, cannot. That you gobbled in
too quick, and though you brought me from a boy
you can make no more of me, only destroy.

Keith Douglas (1920–1944)

RIVERS ARISE

Rivers arise; whether thou be the son
Of utmost Tweed, or Oose, or gulphie Dun,
Or Trent, who like some earth-born giant spreads
His thirty arms among the indented meads,
Or sullen Mole that runneth underneath,
Or Severn swift, guilty of maiden's death,
Or rockie Avon, or of sedgie Lee,
Or coaly Tine, or antient hallowed Dee,
Or Humber loud that keeps the Scythian's name,
Or Medway smooth, or royal towred Thame.

John Milton (1608–1674)

from NIGHT

The sun descending in the west,
The evening star does shine;
The birds are silent in their nest,
And I must seek for mine.
The moon like a flower
In heaven's high bower,
With silent delight
Sits and smiles on the night.

Farewell, green fields and happy groves,
Where flocks have took delight.
Where lambs have nibbled, silent moves
The feet of angels bright;
Unseen they pour blessing
And joy without ceasing,
On each bud and blossom,
And each sleeping bosom.

William Blake (1757–1827)

THE LETTER

From the very first coming down
Into a new valley with a frown
Because of the sun and a lost way,
You certainly remain: to-day
I, crouching behind a sheep-pen, heard
Travel across a sudden bird,
Cry out against the storm, and found
The year's arc a completed round
And love's worn circuit re-begun,
Endless with no dissenting turn.
Shall see, shall pass, as we have seen
The swallow on the tile, spring's green
Preliminary shiver, passed
A solitary truck, the last
Of shunting in the Autumn. But now,
To interrupt the homely brow,
Thought warmed to evening through and through
Your letter comes, speaking as you,
Speaking of much but not to come.

Nor speech is close nor fingers numb,
If love not seldom has received
An unjust answer, was deceived.
I, decent with the seasons, move
Different or with a different love,
Nor question overmuch the nod,
The stone smile of this country god
That never was more reticent,
Always afraid to say more than it meant.

W. H. Auden (1907–1973)

THE FORCE

At Mrs Tyson's farmhouse, the electricity is pumped
Off her beck-borne wooden wheel outside.
Greased, steady, it spins within
A white torrent, that stretches up the rocks.
At night its force bounds down
And shakes the lighted rooms, shakes the light;
The mountain's force comes towering down to us.

High near its summit the brink is hitched
To an overflowing squally tarn.
It trembles with stored storms
That pulse across the rim to us, as light.

On a gusty day like this the force
Lashes its tail, the sky abounds
With wind-stuffed rinds of cloud that sprout
Clear force, throbbing in squalls off the sea
Where the sun stands poring down at itself
And makes the air grow tall in spurts
Whose crests turn over in the night-wind, foaming. We spin
Like a loose wheel, and throbbing shakes our light
Into winter, and torrents dangle. Sun
Pulls up the air in fountains, green shoots, forests
Flinching up at it in spray of branches,
Sends down clear water and the loosened torrent
Down into Mrs Tyson's farmhouse backyard,
That pumps white beams off its crest,
In a stiff breeze lashes its tail down the rocks.

Peter Redgrove (1932–)

143

from **KING LEAR, III, ii**

Another part of the Heath. Storm still.
Enter Lear and Fool.

Lear

Blow, winds, and crack your cheeks! rage! blow!
You cataracts and hurricanoes, spout
Till you have drench'd our steeples, drown'd the cocks!
You sulph'rous and thought-executing fires,
Vaunt-couriers of oak-cleaving thunderbolts,
Singe my white head! And thou, all-shaking thunder,
Strike flat the thick rotundity o' th' world!
Crack Nature's moulds, all germens spill at once
That makes ingrateful man!

Fool

O Nuncle, court holy-water in a dry house is better than this
rain-water out o' door. Good Nuncle, in, ask thy daughters
blessing; here's a night pities neither wise men nor Fools.

Lear

Rumble thy bellyful! Spit, fire! spout, rain!
Nor rain, wind, thunder, fire, are my daughters:
I tax you not, you elements, with unkindness;
I never gave you kingdom, call'd you children,
You owe me no subscription: then let fall
Your horrible pleasure; here I stand, your slave,
A poor, infirm, weak, and despis'd old man.
But yet I call you servile ministers,
That will with two pernicious daughters join
Your high-engender'd battles 'gainst a head
So old and white as this. O, ho! 'tis foul.

William Shakespeare (1564–1616)

BRIGHT STAR! WOULD I WERE
STEADFAST AS THOU ART

Bright star! would I were steadfast as thou art –
  Not in lone splendour hung aloft the night
And watching, with eternal lids apart,
  Like nature's patient, sleepless Eremite,
The moving waters at their priestlike task
  Of pure ablution round earth's human shores,
Or gazing on the new soft-fallen mask
  Of snow upon the mountains and the moors –
No – yet still steadfast, still unchangeable,
  Pillowed upon my fair love's ripening breast,
To feel for ever its soft fall and swell,
  Awake for ever in a sweet unrest,
Still, still to hear her tender-taken breath,
  And so live ever – or else swoon to death.

John Keats (1795–1821)

from TWELFTH NIGHT, V, i

When that I was and a little tiny boy,
   With hey, ho, the wind and the rain;
A foolish thing was but a toy,
   For the rain it raineth every day.

But when I came to man's estate,
   With hey, ho, the wind and the rain;
'Gainst knaves and thieves men shut their gate,
   For the rain it raineth every day.

But when I came, alas! to wive,
   With hey, ho, the wind and the rain;
By swaggering could I never thrive,
   For the rain it raineth every day.

But when I came unto my beds,
   With hey, ho, the wind and the rain;
With toss-pots still had drunken heads,
   For the rain it raineth every day.

A great while ago the world begun,
   With hey, ho, the wind and the rain;
But that's all one, our play is done,
   And we'll strive to please you every day.

William Shakespeare (1564–1616)

RAIN

Rain, midnight rain, nothing but the wild rain
On this bleak hut, and solitude, and me
Remembering again that I shall die
And neither hear the rain nor give it thanks
For washing me cleaner than I have been
Since I was born into this solitude.
Blessed are the dead that the rain rains upon:
But here I pray that none whom once I loved
Is dying to-night or lying still awake
Solitary, listening to the rain,
Either in pain or thus in sympathy
Helpless among the living and the dead,
Like a cold water among broken reeds,
Myriads of broken reeds all still and stiff,
Like me who have no love which this wild rain
Has not dissolved except the love of death,
If love it be for what is perfect and
Cannot, the tempest tells me, disappoint.

Edward Thomas (1878–1917)

ON THE FAIR WEATHER
JUST AT THE CORONATION, IT HAVING RAINED
IMMEDIATELY BEFORE AND AFTER

So clear a season, and so snatch'd from storms,
Shows Heav'n delights to see what Man performs.
Well knew the Sun, if such a day were dim,
It would have been an injury to him:
For then a Cloud had from his eye conceal'd
The noblest sight that ever he beheld.
He therefore check'd th'invading Rains we fear'd,
And in a bright *Parenthesis* appear'd.
So that we knew not which look'd most content,
The King, the People, or the Firmament.
But the Solemnity once fully past,
The storm return'd with an impetuous haste.
And Heav'n and Earth each other to out-do,
Vied both in Cannons and in Fire-works too.
So *Israel* past through the divided flood,
While in obedient heaps the Ocean stood:
But the same sea (the *Hebrews* once on shore)
Return'd in torrents where it was before.

Katherine Philips (1632–1664)

FUTILITY

Move him into the sun –
Gently its touch awoke him once,
At home, whispering of fields unsown.
Always it woke him, even in France,
Until this morning and this snow.
If anything might rouse him now
The kind old sun will know.

Think how it wakes the seeds, –
Woke, once, the clays of a cold star.
Are limbs, so dear-achieved, are sides,
Full-nerved – still warm – too hard to stir?
Was it for this the clay grew tall?
– O what made fatuous sunbeams toil
To break earth's sleep at all?

Wilfred Owen (1893–1918)

ODE TO THE WEST WIND

I

O, wild West Wind, thou breath of Autumn's being,
Thou, from whose unseen presence the leaves dead
Are driven, like ghosts from an enchanter fleeing,

Yellow and black, and pale, and hectic red,
Pestilence-stricken multitudes: O, thou,
Who chariotest to their dark wintry bed

The wingèd seeds, where they lie cold and low,
Each like a corpse within its grave, until
Thine azure sister of the spring shall blow

Her clarion o'er the dreaming earth, and fill
(Driving sweet buds like flocks to feed in air)
With living hues and odours plain and hill:

Wild Spirit, which art moving everywhere:
Destroyer and preserver; hear, O, hear!

II

Thou on whose stream, 'mid the steep sky's commotion,
Loose clouds like earth's decaying leaves are shed,
Shook from the tangled boughs of Heaven and Ocean,

Angels of rain and lightning: there are spread
On the blue surface of thine aëry surge,
Like the bright hair uplifted from the head

Of some fierce Mænad, even from the dim verge
Of the horizon to the zenith's height
The locks of the approaching storm. Thou dirge

Of the dying year, to which this closing night
Will be the dome of a vast sepulchre,
Vaulted with all thy congregated might

Of vapours, from whose solid atmosphere
Black rain, and fire, and hail will burst: O, hear!

III

Thou who didst waken from his summer dreams
The blue Mediterranean, where he lay,
Lulled by the coil of his crystalline streams,

Beside a pumice isle in Baiæ's bay,
And saw in sleep old palaces and towers
Quivering within the wave's intenser day,

All overgrown with azure moss and flowers
So sweet, the sense faints picturing them! Thou
For whose path the Atlantic's level powers

Cleave themselves into chasms, while far below
The sea-blooms and the oozy woods which wear
The sapless foliage of the ocean, know

Thy voice, and suddenly grow grey with fear,
And tremble and despoil themselves: O, hear!

IV

If I were a dead leaf thou mightest bear;
If I were a swift cloud to fly with thee;
A wave to pant beneath thy power, and share

The impulse of thy strength, only less free
Than thou, O, uncontrollable! If even
I were as in my boyhood, and could be

The comrade of thy wanderings over heaven,
As then, when to outstrip thy skiey speed
Scarce seemed a vision; I would ne'er have striven

As thus with thee in prayer in my sore need,
Oh! lift me as a wave, a leaf, a cloud!
I fall upon the thorns of life! I bleed!

A heavy weight of hours has chained and bowed
One too like thee: tameless, and swift, and proud.

V

Make me thy lyre, even as the forest is:
What if my leaves are falling like its own!
The tumult of thy mighty harmonies

Will take from both a deep, autumnal tone,
Sweet though in sadness. Be thou, spirit fierce,
My spirit! Be thou me, impetuous one!

Drive my dead thoughts over the universe
Like withered leaves to quicken a new birth!
And, by the incantation of this verse,

Scatter, as from an unextinguished hearth
Ashes and sparks, my words among mankind!
Be through my lips to unawakened earth

The trumpet of a prophecy! O, wind,
If Winter comes, can Spring be far behind?

Percy Bysshe Shelley (1792–1822)

THE WIND UP THE STREAM

The sheäded stream did run below
Tall elems, on the bank, in row,
That leafy ivy stems did clim'
In light a-shot vrom limb to limb:
An' winds did playÿ, now brisk, now slack,
All up the stream, a-drevèn back
The runnen weäves, an' meäke em seem
To be an upward-flowen stream:
As hope do zometimes meäke us think
Our life do rise, the while do zink.

William Barnes (1801–1886)

SILENCE

Still-born Silence! Thou that art
Flood-gate of the deeper heart!
Offspring of a heavenly kind,
Frost o' th' mouth, and thaw o' th' mind.
Secrecy's confidant and he
Who makes religion mystery!
Admiration's speaking'st tongue!
Leave thy desert shades among
Reverend hermits' hallowed cells,
Where retired Devotion dwells!
With thy enthusiasms come,
Seize our tongues and strike us dumb!

Richard Flecknoe (1600?–1678)

SPRING AND FALL

To a young child

Margaret, are you grieving
Over Goldengrove unleaving?
Leaves, like the things of man, you
With your fresh thoughts care for, can you?
Ah! as the heart grows older
It will come to such sights colder
By and by, nor spare a sigh
Though worlds of wanwood leafmeal lie;
And yet you will weep and know why.
Now no matter, child, the name:
Sorrow's springs are the same.
Nor mouth had, no nor mind, expressed
What heart heard of, ghost guessed:
It is the blight man was born for,
It is Margaret you mourn for.

Gerard Manley Hopkins (1844–1889)

SUMER IS ICUMEN IN

Sing! cuccu, nu. Sing! cuccu.
Sing! cuccu. Sing! cuccu, nu.

Sumer is icumen in –
Lhude sing! cuccu.
Groweth sed and bloweth med
And springth the wude nu –
Sing! cuccu.

Awe bleteth after lomb,
Lhouth after calve cu,
Bulluc sterteth, bucke verteth,
Murie sing! cuccu.
Cuccu, cuccu,
Well singes thu, cuccu –
Ne swik thu naver nu!

Anon (13th Century)

Ne swik thu naver nu! Don't ever stop!

TO AUTUMN

Season of mists and mellow fruitfulness,
    Close bosom-friend of the maturing sun,
Conspiring with him how to load and bless
    With fruit the vines that round the thatch-eves run;
To bend with apples the mossed cottage-trees,
    And fill all fruit with ripeness to the core;
        To swell the gourd, and plump the hazel shells
    With a sweet kernel; to set budding more,
And still more, later flowers for the bees,
Until they think warm days will never cease,
    For Summer has o'er-brimmed their clammy cells.

Who hath not seen thee oft amid thy store?
   Sometimes whoever seeks abroad may find
Thee sitting careless on a granary floor,
   Thy hair soft-lifted by the winnowing wind;
Or on a half-reaped furrow sound asleep,
   Drowsed with the fume of poppies, while thy hook
     Spares the next swath and all its twinèd flowers;
And sometimes like a gleaner thou dost keep
   Steady thy laden head across a brook;
   Or by a cider-press, with patient look,
     Thou watchest the last oozings hours by hours.

Where are the songs of Spring? Ay, where are they?
   Think not of them, thou hast thy music too –
While barrèd clouds bloom the soft-dying day,
   And touch the stubble-plains with rosy hue:
Then in a wailful choir the small gnats mourn
   Among the river sallows, borne aloft
     Or sinking as the light wind lives or dies;
And full-grown lambs loud bleat from hilly bourn;
   Hedge-crickets sing; and now with treble soft
   The redbreast whistles from a garden-croft;
     And gathering swallows twitter in the skies.

John Keats (1795–1821)

from THE SEASONS

WINTER

. . . Drooping, the labourer-ox
Stands covered o'er with snow, and then demands
The fruit of all his toil. The fowls of heaven,
Tamed by the cruel season, crowd around
The winnowing store, and claim the little boon
Which Providence assigns them. One alone,
The redbreast, sacred to the household gods,
Wisely regardful of the embroiling sky,
In joyless fields and thorny thickets leaves
His shivering mates, and pays to trusted man
His annual visit. Half afraid, he first
Against the window beats; then brisk alights
On the warm hearth; then hopping o'er the floor,
Eyes all the smiling family askance,
And pecks, and starts, and wonders where he is –
Till more familiar grown, the table-crumbs
Attract his slender feet. The foodless wilds
Pour forth their brown inhabitants. The hare,
Though timorous of heart, and hard beset
By death in various forms, dark snares, and dogs,
And more unpitying men, the garden seeks,
Urged on by fearless want. The bleating kind
Eye the bleak heaven, and next the glistening earth,
With looks of dumb despair; then, sad-dispersed,
Dig for the withered herb through heaps of snow.

James Thomson (1700–1748)

GOD SPEDE THE PLOW

The merthe of all this londe
Maketh the gode husbonde
With ering of his plow;
Yblessed be Cristes sonde
That hath us sent in honde
Merthe and joy ynow.

The plow goth mony a gate
Both erly and eke late
In winter in the clay
About barly and whete,
That maketh men to swete.
God spede the plow all day!

Brown, Morel and Gore
Drawen the plow full sore
All in the morwening;
Rewarde hem therfore
With a shefe or more
All in the evening.

Whan men begin to sowe
Full well her corn they knowe
In the month of May.
How ever Janiver blowe,
Whether hye or lowe,
God spede the plow all way!

Whan men beginneth to wede
The thistle fro the sede,
In somer whan they may.
God let hem well to spede:
And long good life to lede,
All that for plowmen pray.

Anon (15th Century)

ering ploughing *gate* way

158

NO!

No sun – no moon!
No morn – no noon –
No dawn – no dusk – no proper time of day –
  No sky – no earthly view –
  No distance looking blue –
No road – no street – no 't'other side the way' –
  No end to any Row –
  No indications where the Crescents go –
  No top to any steeple –
No recognitions of familiar people –
  No courtesies for showing 'em –
  No knowing 'em!
No travelling at all – no locomotion,
No inkling of the way – no notion –
  'No go' – by land or ocean –
  No mail – no post –
No news from any foreign coast –
No Park – no Ring – no afternoon gentility –
  No company – no nobility –
No warmth, no cheerfulness, no healthful ease,
  No comfortable feel in any member –
No shade, no shine, no butterflies, no bees,
  No fruits, no flowers, no leaves, no birds –
    November!

Thomas Hood (1799–1845)

THIS WORLD'S JOY

Winter wakeneth all my care,
Now these leaves waxen bare;
Oft I sigh and mourne sair
    When it cometh in my thought
    Of this world's joy, how it goeth all to nought.

Now it is and now it nis,
All as it ne'er were, I wis;
That many men say, sooth it is:
    All goeth, but God's will,
    All we shall die, though us like ill.

All that green me grieveth green,
Now it faleweth albydene:
Jesu, help that it be seen,
    And shield us from hell!
    For I not whither I shall, nor how long here dwell.

Anon (15th Century)

faleweth albydene fades completely

from LOVE'S LABOUR'S LOST, V, ii

SPRING

When daisies pied and violets blue
   And lady-smocks all silver-white
And cuckoo-buds of yellow hue
   Do paint the meadows with delight,
The cuckoo then, on every tree,
Mocks married men; for thus sings he,
                 'Cuckoo!
Cuckoo, cuckoo!' O word of fear,
Unpleasing to a married ear!

When shepherds pipe on oaten straws,
   And merry larks are ploughman's clocks,
When turtles tread, and rooks and daws,
   And maidens bleach their summer smocks,
The cuckoo then, on every tree,
Mocks married men; for thus sings he,
                 'Cuckoo!
Cuckoo, cuckoo!' O word of fear,
Unpleasing to a married ear!

WINTER

When icicles hang by the wall,
   And Dick the shepherd blows his nail,
And Tom bears logs into the hall,
   And milk comes frozen home in pail;
When blood is nipped, and ways be foul,
Then nightly sings the staring owl
   'Tu-whit, to-whoo!' A merry note,
While greasy Joan doth keel the pot.

When all around the wind doth blow,
    And coughing drowns the parson's saw,
And birds sit brooding in the snow,
    And Marian's nose looks red and raw;
When roasted crabs hiss in the bowl,
Then nightly sings the staring owl
    'Tu-whit, to-whoo!' A merry note,
While greasy Joan doth keel the pot.

William Shakespeare (1564–1616)

TO HIS HONOURED FRIEND,
MR GILES BALLE, MERCHANT

The lofty mountains standing on a row,
Which but of late were periwigged with snow,
Doff off their coats, and now are daily seen
To stand on tiptoes, all in swaggering green.
Meadows and gardens are pranked up with buds
And chirping birds now chant it in the woods,
The warbling swallow and the lark do sing,
To welcome in the glorious, verdant Spring.

Robert Chamberlain (1607–?)

from BURLESQUE UPON THE GREAT FROST

But, to leave fooling, I assure ye
There never was so cold a fury
Of nipping frost, and pinching weather
Since Eve and Adam met together.
Our Peak, that always has been famous
For cold wherewith to cramp and lame us,
Worse than itself, did now resemble a
Certain damn'd place call'd Nova Zembla,
And we who boast us human creatures,
Had happy been had we chang'd features,
Garments at least, though theirs be shabbed,
With those who that cold place inhabit,
The bears and foxes, who *sans* question
Than we by odds have warmer vests on.
How cold that country is, he knows most
Has there his fingers and his toes lost;
But here I know that every member
Alike was handled by December;
Who blew his nose had clout or fist all
Instead of snivel fill'd with crystal,
Who drew for urinal ejection,
Was bewitched into an odd erection,
And these, Priapus like, stood strutting,
Fitter for pedestal than rutting:
As men were fierce, or gentle handed,
Their fists were clutch'd or palms expanded,
Limbs were extended, or contracted,
As use or humour most affected;
For, as men did to th'air expose 'em,
It catch'd and in that figure froze 'em . . .

Charles Cotton (1630–1686)

163

HOME-THOUGHTS, FROM ABROAD

Oh to be in England
Now that April's there,
And whoever wakes in England
Sees, some morning, unaware,
That the lowest boughs and the brushwood sheaf
Round the elm-tree bole are in tiny leaf,
While the chaffinch sings on the orchard bough
In England – now!

And after April, when May follows,
And the whitethroat builds, and all the swallows!
Hark! where my blossomed pear-tree in the hedge
Leans to the field and scatters on the clover
Blossoms and dewdrops – at the bent spray's edge –
That's the wise thrush; he sings each song twice over,
Lest you should think he never could recapture
The first fine careless rapture!
And though the fields look rough with hoary dew,
All will be gay when noontide wakes anew
The buttercups, the little children's dower
– Far brighter than this gaudy melon–flower!

Robert Browning (1812–1889)

HURRAHING IN HARVEST

Summer ends now; now, barbarous in beauty, the stooks arise
   Around; up above, what wind-walks! what lovely behaviour
   Of silk-sack clouds! has wilder, wilful-wavier
Meal-drift moulded ever and melted across skies?

I walk, I lift up, I lift up heart, eyes,
   Down all that glory in the heavens to glean our Saviour;
   And, eyes, heart, what looks, what lips yet gave you a
Rapturous love's greeting of realer, of rounder replies?

And the azurous hung hills are his world-wielding shoulder
   Majestic – as a stallion stalwart, very-violet-sweet! –
These things, these things were here and but the beholder
   Wanting; which two when they once meet,
The heart rears wings bold and bolder
   And hurls for him, O half hurls earth for him off under
     his feet.

Gerard Manley Hopkins (1844–1889)

from A MIDSUMMER NIGHT'S DREAM, II, i

Titania
   And never, since the middle summer's spring,
   Met we on hill, in dale, forest, or mead,
   By pavèd fountain or by rushy brook,
   Or in the beachèd margent of the sea,
   To dance our ringlets to the whistling wind,
   But with thy brawls thou hast disturbed our sport.
   Therefore the winds, piping to us in vain,
   As in revenge, have sucked up from the sea
   Contagious fogs; which, falling in the land,

Hath every pelting river made so proud
That they have overborne their continents.
The ox hath therefore stretched his yoke in vain,
The plowman lost his sweat, and the green corn
Hath rotted ere his youth attained a beard;
The fold stands empty in the drownèd field,
And crows are fatted with the murrion flock;
The nine men's morris is filled up with mud;
And the quaint mazes in the wanton green,
For lack of tread, are undistinguishable.
The human mortals want their winter here;
No night is now with hymn or carol blest.
Therefore the moon, the governess of floods,
Pale in her anger, washes all the air,
That rheumatic diseases do abound.
And thorough this distemperature we see
The seasons alter: hoary-headed frosts
Fall in the fresh lap of the crimson rose,
And on old Hiems' thin and icy crown
An odorous chaplet of sweet summer buds
Is, as in mockery, set. The spring, the summer,
The childing autumn, angry winter, change
Their wanton liveries; and the mazèd world,
By their increase, now knows not which is which.
And this same progeny of evils comes
From our debate, from our dissension;
We are their parents and original.

William Shakespeare (1564–1616)

FLOWERS, PLANTS AND TREES

Sweet spring, full of sweet days and roses,
A box where sweets compacted lie . . .

George Herbert, 'Virtue'

The sky has its birds, clouds and rushing currents of air; earth has flowers, trees, plants and herbs. Experts know all the varieties and rules of propagation, the rest of us commune with them in our own inarticulate way. Daily life would be inconceivable without their vegetable presence, an alternative mode of being to ours, symbolising intangible states of mind, the incarnation of beauty.

Chaucer loved the humble daisy, which he saw, paradoxically, as empress of the meadows. Spenser's 'flowery meads' lying alongside the 'sweet Thames' comfort the disillusioned courtier in 'Prothalamion'. Shakespeare, Milton, Wordsworth all home in on the violet. Shelley wonders what woman can possibly be worthy of this natural language of love. Many flowers' names are a poem in themselves – lily, amaranthus, daffodil, pansy, chrysanthemum, eglantine, hollyhock, foxglove. Maybe the genius of the language lies in such names, and all a poet has to do is pick from that abundance.

Trees are bigger, tougher, more assertive, both 'armies' and 'temples'. 'I see men as trees walking' says Keith Douglas in 'Desert Flowers'. Herbs have their own lore, as any herbal testifies. Grass, rushes, weeds – those disenfranchised flowers – and all their cousins and declensions are yet another world unto themselves, 'pricking my ankles and murmuring of their humility' as Sylvia Plath says in 'The Moon and the Yew Tree'. Or putting our humility in its place.

168

VIRTUE

Sweet day, so cool, so calm, so bright,
The bridal of the earth and sky:
The dew shall weep thy fall tonight;
    For thou must die.

Sweet rose, whose hue angry and brave
Bids the rash gazer wipe his eye:
Thy root is ever in its grave,
    And thou must die.

Sweet spring, full of sweet days and roses,
A box where sweets compacted lie;
My music shows ye have your closes,
    And all must die.

Only a sweet and virtuous soul,
Like season'd timber, never gives;
But though the whole world turns to coal,
    Then chiefly lives.

George Herbert (1593–1633)

THE SICK ROSE

O Rose, thou art sick!
The invisible worm
That flies in the night,
In the howling storm,

Has found out thy bed
Of crimson joy:
And his dark secret love
Does thy life destroy.

William Blake (1757–1827)

from A MIDSUMMER NIGHT'S DREAM, II, i

Oberon

Yet markt I where the bolt of Cupid fell:
It fell upon a little western flower,
Before milk-white, now purple with love's wound,
And maidens call it love-in-idleness.
Fetch me that flower; the herb I shew'd thee once:
The juice of it on sleeping eyelids laid
Will make or man or woman madly dote
Upon the next live creature that it sees.
Fetch me this herb; and be thou here again
Ere the leviathan can swim a league.

Puck

I'll put a girdle round about the earth
In forty minutes.

*   *   *

Oberon

I know a bank where the wild thyme blows,
Where oxlips and the nodding violet grows,

Quite overcanopied with luscious woodbine,
With sweet musk roses, and with eglantine.
There sleeps Titania sometime of the night,
Lulled in these flowers with dances and delight;
And there the snake throws her enameled skin,
Weed wide enough to wrap a fairy in.
And with the juice of this I'll streak her eyes,
And make her full of hateful fantasies.

William Shakespeare (1564–1616)

TO DAFFODILS

Fair Daffodils, we weep to see
    You haste away so soon:
As yet the early-rising sun
    Has not attained his noon.
     Stay, stay,
    Until the hasting day
     Has run
    But to the even-song;
And, having prayed together, we
    Will go with you along.

We have short time to stay as you,
    We have as short a spring;
As quick, a growth to meet decay
    As you, or any thing.
     We die
    As your hours do, and dry
     Away
    Like to the summer's rain;
Or as the pearls of morning's dew,
    Ne'er to be found again.

Robert Herrick (1591–1674)

from **A WINTER'S TALE, IV, iv**

Perdita

    Here's flowers for you:
    Hot lavender, mints, savory, marjoram,
    The marigold, that goes to bed wi' th' Sun,
    And with him rises, weeping: these are flowers
    Of middle summer, and I think they are given
    To men of middle age. You're very welcome.

Camillo

    I should leave grazing, were I of your flock,
    And only live by gazing.

Perdita

    . . . Now, my fair'st friend,
    I would I had some flowers o' th' Spring, that might
    Become your time of day: and yours, and yours,
    That wear upon your virgin branches yet
    Your maidenheads growing: O Proserpina,
    For the flowers now, that (frighted) thou let'st fall
    From Dis's waggon: daffodils,
    That come before the swallow dares, and take
    The winds of March with beauty: violets (dim,
    But sweeter than the lids of Juno's eyes,
    Or Cytherea's breath), pale prime-roses,
    That die unmarried, ere they can behold
    Bright Phœbus in his strength (a malady
    Most incident to maids): bold oxlips, and
    The crown imperial: lilies of all kinds,
    (The flower-de-luce being one). O, these I lack,
    To make you garlands of, and my sweet friend,
    To strew him o'er and o'er.

Florizel

    What? like a corse?

Perdita
No, like a bank, for Love to lie, and play on:
Not like a corse: or if: not to be buried,
But quick, and in mine arms.

William Shakespeare (1564–1616)

A CONTEMPLATION UPON FLOWERS

Brave flowers – that I could gallant it like you,
    And be as little vain!
You come abroad, and make a harmless show,
    And to your beds of earth again.
You are not proud: you know your birth:
For your embroidered garments are from earth.

You do obey your months and times, but I
    Would have it ever Spring:
My fate would know no Winter, never die,
    Nor think of such a thing.
O that I could my bed of earth but view
And smile, and look as cheerfully as you!

O teach me to see Death and not to fear,
    But rather to take truce!
How often have I seen you at a bier,
    And there look fresh and spruce.
You fragrant flowers! Then teach me, that my breath
Like yours may sweeten and perfume my death.

Henry King (1592–1669)

from LYCIDAS

. . . Throw hither all your quaint enamelled eyes,
That on the green turf suck the honied showers,
And purple all the ground with vernal flowers.
Bring the rathe primrose that forsaken dies,
The tufted crow-toe, and pale jessamine,
The white pink, and the pansy freaked with jet,
The glowing violet,
The musk rose, and the well-attired woodbine,
With cowslips wan that hang the pensive head,
And every flower that sad embroidery wears.
Bid amaranthus all his beauty shed,
And daffadillies fill their cups with tears,
To strew the laureate hearse where Lycid lies.
For so to interpose a little ease,
Let our frail thoughts dally with false surmise;
Ay me! whilst thee the shores and sounding seas
Wash far away, where'er thy bones are hurled,
Whether beyond the stormy Hebrides,
Where thou perhaps under the whelming tide
Visit'st the bottom of the monstrous world;
Or whether thou, to our moist vows denied,
Sleep'st by the fable of Bellerus old,
Where the great Vision of the guarded mount
Looks towards Namancos, and Bayona's hold.
Look homeward, Angel, now, and melt with ruth:
And, O ye dolphins, waft the hapless youth.

John Milton (1608–1674)

THE QUESTION

I dreamed that, as I wandered by the way,
   Bare winter suddenly was changed to spring,
And gentle odours led my steps astray,
   Mixed with a sound of waters murmuring
Along a shelving bank of turf, which lay
   Under a copse, and hardly dared to fling
Its green arms round the bosom of the stream,
But kissed it and then fled, as thou mightest in dream.

There grew pied wind-flowers and violets,
   Daisies, those pearled Arcturi of the earth,
The constellated flower that never sets;
   Faint oxlips; tender bluebells, at whose birth
The sod scarce heaved; and that tall flower that wets
   (Like a child, half in tenderness and mirth)
Its mother's face with heaven-collected tears,
When the low wind, its playmate's voice, it hears.

And in the warm hedge grew lush eglantine,
   Green cowbind and the moonlight-coloured May,
And cherry-blossoms, and white cups, whose wine
   Was the bright dew, yet drained not by the day;
And wild roses, and ivy serpentine,
   With its dark buds and leaves, wandering astray;
And flowers azure, black, and streaked with gold,
Fairer than any wakened eyes behold.

And nearer to the river's trembling edge
   There grew broad flag-flowers, purple prankt with white,
And starry river-buds among the sedge,
   And floating water-lilies, broad and bright,
Which hit the oak that overhung the hedge
   With moonlight beams of their own watery light;
And bulrushes and reeds of such deep green
As soothed the dazzled eye with sober sheen.

Methought that of these visionary flowers
    I made a nosegay, bound in such a way
That the same hues, which in their natural bowers
    Were mingled or opposed, the like array
Kept these imprisoned children of the Hours
    Within my hand, – and then, elate and gay,
I hastened to the spot whence I had come,
That I might there present it! – oh! to whom?

Percy Bysshe Shelley (1782–1822)

THE WOODSPURGE

The wind flapped loose, the wind was still,
Shaken out dead from tree and hill;
I had walked on at the wind's will, –
I sat now, for the wind was still.

Between my knees my forehead was, –
My lips, drawn in, said not Alas!
My hair was over in the grass,
My naked ears heard the day pass.

My eyes, wide open, had the run
Of some ten weeds to fix upon;
Among those few, out of the sun,
The woodspurge flowered, three cups in one.

From perfect grief there need not be
Wisdom or even memory:
One thing then learnt remains to me, –
The woodspurge has a cup of three.

Dante Gabriel Rossetti (1828–1882)

from THE LEGEND OF GOOD WOMEN

THE DAISY

And Zepherus and Flora gentilly
Yaf to the floures, softe and tenderly,
Hire swoote breth, and made hem for to sprede,
As god and goddesse of the floury mede;
In which me thoghte I myghte, day by day,
Duellen alwey, the joly month of May,
Withouten slep, withouten mete or drynke.
Adoun ful softely I gan to synke,
And lenynge on myn elbowe and my syde,
The longe day I shoop me for t'abide
For nothing elles, and I shal nat lye,
But for to loke upon the dayesie,
That wel by reson men it calle may
The 'dayesye,' or elles the 'ye of day,'
The emperice and flour of floures alle.
I pray to God that faire mote she falle,
And alle that loven floures, for hire sake!

Geoffrey Chaucer (1340?–1400)

DANDELIONS

Incorrigible, brash,
They brightened the cinder path of my childhood,
Unsubtle, the opposite of primroses,
But, unlike primroses, capable
Of growing anywhere, railway track, pierhead,
Like our extrovert friends who never
Make us fall in love, yet fill
The primroseless roseless gaps.

Louis MacNeice (1907–1963)

ON HIS MISTRESS' GARDEN OF HERBS

Heart's-ease, a herb that sometimes hath been seen
In my love's garden plot, to flourish green,
Is dead and withered with a wind of woe;
And bitter rue in place thereof doth grow.
The cause I find to be, because I did
Neglect the herb called Time: which now doth bid
Me never hope; nor look once more again
To gain heart's-ease, to ease my heart of pain.
One hope is this, in this my woeful case,
My rue, though bitter, may prove herb of grace.

Anon (17th Century)

OLD MAN

Old Man, or Lad's-love, – in the name there's nothing
To one that knows not Lad's-love, or Old Man,
The hoar-green feathery herb, almost a tree,
Growing with rosemary and lavender.
Even to one that knows it well, the names
Half decorate, half perplex, the thing it is:
At least, what that is clings not to the names
In spite of time. And yet I like the names.

The herb itself I like not, but for certain
I love it, as some day the child will love it
Who plucks a feather from the door-side bush
Whenever she goes in or out of the house.
Often she waits there, snipping the tips and shrivelling
The shreds at last on to the path, perhaps
Thinking, perhaps of nothing, till she sniffs
Her fingers and runs off. The bush is still
But half as tall as she, though it is as old;

So well she clips it. Not a word she says;
And I can only wonder how much hereafter
She will remember, with that bitter scent,
Of garden rows, and ancient damson trees
Topping a hedge, a bent path to a door,
A low thick bush beside the door, and me
Forbidding her to pick.
                              As for myself,
Where first I met the bitter scent is lost.
I, too, often shrivel the grey shreds,
Sniff them and think and sniff again and try
Once more to think what it is I am remembering,
Always in vain. I cannot like the scent,
Yet I would rather give up others more sweet,
With no meaning, than this bitter one.

I have mislaid the key. I sniff the spray
And think of nothing; I see and I hear nothing;
Yet seem, too, to be listening, lying in wait
For what I should, yet never can, remember:
No garden appears, no path, no hoar-green bush
Of Lad's-love, or Old Man, no child beside,
Neither father nor mother, nor any playmate;
Only an avenue, dark, nameless, without end.

Edward Thomas (1878–1917)

PRIVET

Clipped privet, deprived of pride,
The shears assume you are nothing but hedge.
Hold up your ovals, take rain for a ride,
Parade your smart at the road's edge.

Christopher Pilling (1936–)

THISTLES

Against the rubber tongues of cows and the hoeing hands of men
Thistles spike the summer air
Or crackle open under a blue-black pressure.

Every one a revengeful burst
Of resurrection, a grasped fistful
Of splintered weapons and Icelandic frost thrust up

From the underground stain of a decayed Viking.
They are like pale hair and the gutturals of dialects.
Every one manages a plume of blood.

Then they grow grey, like men.
Mown down, it is a feud. Their sons appear,
Stiff with weapons, fighting back over the same ground.

Ted Hughes (1930–)

TALL NETTLES

Tall nettles cover up, as they have done
These many springs, the rusty harrow, the plough
Long worn out, and the roller made of stone:
Only the elm butt tops the nettles now.

This corner of the farmyard I like most:
As well as any bloom upon a flower
I like the dust on the nettles, never lost
Except to prove the sweetness of a shower.

Edward Thomas (1878–1917)

from THE TIMBER

Sure thou didst flourish once! and many springs,
   Many bright mornings, much dew, many showers,
Passed o'er thy head; many light hearts and wings,
   Which now are dead, lodged in thy living bowers.

And still a new succession sings and flies;
   Fresh groves grow up, and their green branches shoot
Towards the old and still enduring skies,
   While the low violet thrives at their root.

But thou beneath the sad and heavy line
   Of death, doth waste all senseless, cold, and dark,
Where not so much as dreams of light may shine,
   Nor any thought of greenness, leaf or bark.

And yet – as if some deep hate and dissent,
   Bred in thy growth betwixt high winds and thee,
Were still alive – thou dost great storms resent
   Before they come, and know'st how near they be.

Else all at rest thou liest, and the fierce breath
   Of tempests can no more disturb thy ease;
But this thy strange resentment after death
   Means only those who broke – in life – thy peace.

Henry Vaughan (1621–1695)

LARCH TREES

Cumberland

All men speak ill of thee, unlucky Tree!
   Spoiling with graceless line the mountain edge,
   Clothing with awkward sameness rifted ledge,
Or uplands swelling brokenly and free:
Yet shalt thou win some few good words of me.
   Thy boughs it is that teach the wind to mourn,
   Haunting deep inland spots and groves forlorn
With the true murmurs of the plaintive sea.
When tuft and shoot on vernal woodlands shine,
Who hath a green unwinterlike as thine?
And when thou leanest o'er some beetling brow,
   With pale thin twigs the eye can wander through,
There is no other tree on earth but thou
   Which brings the sky so near or makes it seem so blue.

Reverend F. W. Faber (1814–1863)

YEW-TREES

There is a Yew-tree, pride of Lorton Vale,
Which to this day stands single, in the midst
Of its own darkness, as it stood of yore,
Not loth to furnish weapons for the Bands
Of Umfraville or Percy ere they marched
To Scotland's Heaths; or Those that crossed the Sea
And drew their sounding bows at Azincour,
Perhaps at earlier Crecy, or Poictiers.
Of vast circumference and gloom profound
This solitary Tree! – a living thing
Produced too slowly ever to decay;

Of form and aspect too magnificent
To be destroyed. But worthier still of note
Are those fraternal Four of Borrowdale,
Joined in one solemn and capacious grove;
Huge trunks! – and each particular trunk a growth
Of intertwisted fibres serpentine
Up-coiling, and inveterately convolved, –
Nor uninformed with Phantasy, and looks
That threaten the prophane; – a pillared shade,
Upon whose grassless floor of red-brown hue,
By sheddings from the pining umbrage tinged
Perennially – beneath whose sable roof
Of boughs, as if for festal purpose, decked
With unrejoicing berries, ghostly Shapes
May meet at noontide – Fear and trembling Hope,
Silence and Foresight – Death the Skeleton
And Time the Shadow, – there to celebrate,
As in a natural temple scattered o'er
With altars undisturbed of mossy stone,
United worship; or in mute repose
To lie, and listen to the mountain flood
Murmuring from Glaramara's inmost caves.

William Wordsworth (1770–1850)

THE ONE DESIRE

The palm-house in Belfast's Botanic Gardens
Was built before Kew
In the spirit that means to outdo
The modern by the more modern,

That iron be beaten, and glass
Bent to our will,
That heaven be brought closer still
And we converse with the angels.

The palm-house has now run to seed;
Rusting girders, a missing pane
Through which some delicate tree
Led by kindly light
Would seem at last to have broken through.
We have excelled ourselves again.

Paul Muldoon (1951–)

A SHROPSHIRE LAD

II

Loveliest of trees, the cherry now
Is hung with bloom along the bough,
And stands about the woodland ride
Wearing white for Eastertide.

Now, of my threescore years and ten,
Twenty will not come again,
And take from seventy springs a score,
It only leaves me fifty more.

And since to look at things in bloom
Fifty springs are little room,
About the woodlands I will go
To see the cherry hung with snow.

A. E. Housman (1859–1936)

INDEX OF POETS

187

INDEX OF FIRST LINES